To Live with Hope

To Live with Hope

G. Temp Sparkman

Illustrated by Catherine Kunz

Judson Press® Valley Forge

Library of Congress Cataloging in Publication Data
Sparkman, G. Temp.
    To live with hope.

    1. Meditations. 2. Sparkman, G. Temp. I. Title.
BV4832.2.S67 1985   242   84-21766
ISBN 0-8170-1062-9

*To Teresa Elizabeth and Jennifer Lynn
who in the death of their middle sister Laura Suzanna
unwittingly modeled hoping.*

Contents

**Overture
to Hope**

Overture to Hope

In the soft dusk of a summer evening a butterfly frolicked in the remaining light. I watched it for a while by earth time, by primal measure a timeless period, as it celebrated wind and light, sky and earth. Other eyes were fixed on the colorful creature's delight in the given instant. A blue jay, bowered in a nearby maple, watched, and as if under threat, winged swiftly toward the unaware butterfly, striking it on the wing. The helpless butterfly dipped, attempted a recovery, then fell to the grass between my feet. Its variegated wing partially torn away, the lovely creature fluttered a mild appeal for me to repair its misfortune, then died quietly. Inept in the face of the event before me, I protested that the butterfly had spent the winter in the chrysalis for its mysterious metamorphosis to come to such an ignoble end. I cursed the jay for its capricious violence. In the hushed terror of that moment an old lesson came back to mind: Nothing is permanent.

The preacher stepped confidently to his station and, addressing the somber congregation, proclaimed, "It is a happy day; our brother has gone to be with the Lord." If the minister spoke truth, then why the introspective stares from among the pews? Why the ashen faces and quivering lips from the family on the front row? Although most of the mourners probably believed in earnest that their brother was indeed now with God, no one appeared as convinced as the smiling preacher that it was a happy day. Can it be that the self-examination and the sobriety represent, in a measure, our experiencing of our own demise? Can it be that in such moments we are facing the certainty that we, too, as Walter Chalmers Smith wrote, ". . . blossom and flourish as leaves on the tree," and, as inevitably, "wither and perish."[1] Nothing is permanent.

In a brief span of years the telephone lines across the miles have borne the unwelcomed, sometimes shocking, sometimes expected news of the deaths of four members of my family—Tom, Joe, Cooper, and Carpie—and of a dear friend, Grady Nutt. My eyes have been drawn to the pages of newspapers reporting the deaths of a spiritual model, Abraham Heschel; a professional hero, W. L. Howse; and an integrity model, Carlyle Marney. Two colleagues, B. A. Sizemore and Clifford Ingle, have died. I have rushed to the side of friends in the deaths of Nancy Hankins and Jo Catherine Ferguson, children gone, as flowers cut before the bloom. For most of these dead, I was among the mourners at the graveside. In each case, the open grave was set in a wide expanse of sealed graves, some new, some guarded by weather-worn rocks, some bearing familiar names. As I scanned the panorama of crosses before me, my heart felt the words of Isaac Watts, "Time, like an ever-rolling stream, Bears all its sons away."[2] All is transient.

On a snowy Saturday in a January of some years ago, an innocent and beautiful child lay victim of an undeserved, devastating disease which she had fought with uncommon courage for almost two years. She could resist no longer, nor could the giving love of her parents and the hopeful prayers of many keep her from the ravages of her awful affliction. I held with her mother and her father, my colleague in ministry, "It makes no sense. It makes no sense."

As one of my children entered adolescence she answered a telephone call to hear from a friend, "I am in the hospital." They made friend talk for almost an hour, then my daughter turned to ready her things for tomorrow's school; her friend, to uncertainty. In a few days the diagnosis was in; it was not good. My daughter watched her friend bear an "outrageous fortune." We all experienced again the bewilderment of absurdity. I held with her mother and her father, "It makes no sense."

When I was a child, my days defined by school and play,

there was an evil loose in Europe, at first unknown to the rest of the world. Gradually the word about our brothers and sisters in the gas ovens became known to the outside. It was incredible but true. The Jews were being systematically exterminated. In my childhood, I heard it as sad news and experienced it as melancholy. In my adulthood, with innocence lost, I hear it for the inconceivable, terrifying tragedy that it is, was—no, is. I experience it as a deep wound.

As with other mass deaths in our century in Russia and Cambodia, we are face to face with stark absurdities. We find no rational explanation, no fragment of reason in them that approximates any sense of purpose. At least in war, though its battleground is hell, we can attempt to name a reason that places its insanity within some perspective that approaches purpose. But the tragedy of holocaust past and its prospect in nuclear war fit into no mental scheme, find home in no vision for humanity. Away from the day's distractions, I ponder that. I admit to an inner terror of the tragic.

A woman seminary student asked to talk with me after a Tuesday morning class. Her eyes looked troubled and, in my office, yielded tears. The church of which she is a member was without a minister of education, and she, about to complete her master's degree, applied for the job. She was told that although she had the respect of the church and was qualified for the job, she could not be elected because she is a woman. My heart and eyes matched the heaviness and the tears of her eyes. What an injustice!

The noble and inspiring life of Martin Luther King, Jr., was ended much too early. His killer occupies a prison cubicle and waits out his pitiful and unproductive existence. In a time farther removed, two prisoners of the state, who held in common only that they were children of God and guilty in the eyes of the law, stood before a howling crowd. "Which prisoner will you have," the ruler asked, "Jesus or Barabbas?" It is admittedly an overstatement, but there is enough truth in it for it to be repeated: There is no justice in this world.

13

Hoping is born in us when we stand at the mercy of the impermanent, the irrational, and the unjust. Hoping is set against the trauma and bewilderment of the transient, the absurd, the unjust. "Hoping" is a neutral word like "feeling" or "thinking." However, it may be evoked in a religious or nonreligious setting.

The neutrality of hoping is evident in the experience of the existentialist. If the character of existence is of the genre of Sartre's judgment that "hell is other people," then the person caught in such despair will hope for early deliverance. As substance, the hope is for annihilation, thus for freedom from the imprisoning now.

In the religious context, the activity we call hoping remains neutral, but hope is, in its content, religious. Thus may we speak meaningfully of the hope of our hope. For the Hebrews, vassals in Egypt, hope was a religious reality. It was Yahweh who sent Moses to the pharaoh with the words that made hope real: "Let my people go." In early Christian literature hope was not religiously neutral: "We hope for a city whose builder is God."

Against the milieu of impermanence, absurdity, and injustice, hoping appears. The substance of hope is elsewhere, but hope's womb is the exigencies of living. When there is no explanation, no solution, no balm in the event, we can hope. When we cannot bring back to warm communion those who have died, we can hope. When we cannot reverse the obscene injustices of this world, we can hope. When we cannot, for and in ourselves, fend off injustice, escape the absurd, or assure our own permanence, we can hope.

And so I do. I live in hope. What follows is my journey. I am going back down its path of some years. As the poet bade, "—You come too."

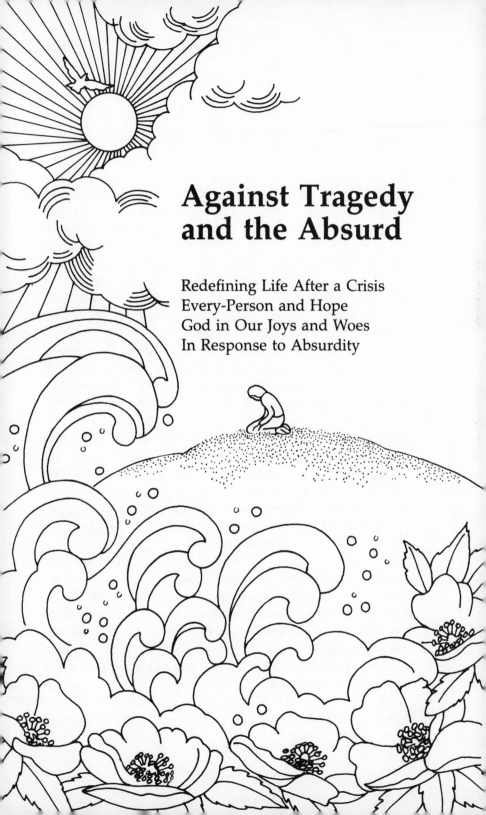

Against Tragedy and the Absurd

Redefining Life After a Crisis
Every-Person and Hope
God in Our Joys and Woes
In Response to Absurdity

Redefining Life After a Crisis

In a recent Saturday's twilight Jennifer, my six-year-old daughter, and I were playing in the new sandbox I had built for the children. We were pretending to be making a tiered, oriental garden, with a pool at the bottom of the hill. The sand was just damp enough for us to manage it well, and our garden was lovely, partly, of course, in our imagination. I had done the landscaping with a miniature shovel, and Jennifer had created the shrubbery with a small plastic cup. Jennifer liked our creation so much that she had an idea. "Let's put a top on the sandbox so that what we made won't get torn down." I told her that that is not the way it is with sandboxes, that what you do is create what you can while you are playing; then if your work is destroyed, you start over again.

In our family we thought there would always be the five of us, though we knew that time and circumstance would scatter us. Then, one summer, haughty death stalked across our dreams and we stood, helpless, as Laura Suzanna died. It was as if we were bound, watching a thief take a prized possession. There was absolutely nothing we could do but reassure her of our love and of God's.

We were not the first to experience the death of a growing and happy child. Many of you have stood right where we stood, and you know how shaky the ground becomes.

And death is not the only crisis that cuts across our dreams to leave us stunned. There may not be in all of earth's realities a more beautiful moment than when a man and a woman decide that in marriage they will begin making a new life together. Then, sometimes early, sometimes after years of companionship, sometimes before children are born into the home, sometimes afterward, that moment, born in a dream

16

of love and joy, is shattered. The causes are innumerable and complex, but the effect is the same.

Robert Frost wrote a poem, "The Hill Wife," about a woman who had no children and nothing much to do except follow her husband while he plowed the fields. One day she slipped off into the woods and never returned. She heard her husband call but did not answer. Then, said Frost of the man, he learned about separations other than death.

But death and divorce are not the only crises. Young men and young women dream dreams about careers; they study and work hard; they find themselves in the work they want to do; but eventually disillusionment enters their experience, coming from a thousand directions. These critical periods may be attributed to unreal expectations about the job, a mismatch of one's ability and job requirements, interpersonal conflicts or a head-on collision with power. Whatever the cause, these persons find themselves in their middle years with their childhood dreams far removed.

There are, of course, many other events that are major crises. There is political defeat; there are defective decisions which have caused pain and alienation; there are broken relationships; there is suddenly in one's home a disabled child or mate, or a terminal disease; and there are a seemingly endless number of other physical and psychological crises. We all face them. There is no way to avoid some of these crises, and I suppose that all of us live with some measure of the dynamics of most of life's crises.

Since we cannot escape the pain that comes with being a part of the human family, we have to find some way of getting hold of ourselves, some way of living with the pain. As long as there is life, there is the possibility of getting hold of some tangible aspect of the crisis that we face, and of doing something about it.

In the case of my family, the point at which we wanted to get hold of the crisis was closed to us. We wanted to help Laura survive the onslaught of the disease, and we did this

17

through some excellent doctors and nurses. But the limitations of medical technology were such that we were forced at last to confront the unalterable reality of her separation from us.

At first our job was to work through the initial shock that something like this could happen to so healthy and joyful a child. Perhaps it is too much to say we worked through this period. It is more as if we were carried through it, for we were hardly conscious enough to work at anything. Still, there were necessary decisions that had to be made the very morning of her death. It seemed like such an unreal moment, for we were having to speak the same information about her that we had given when she registered for school, and swimming lessons, and all those other happy childhood activities. But it was real, irreversibly real, and by nightfall with Jennifer and Teresa in from play, the grief was smothering, and Faye and I learned that there are times when faith is just a deep breath.

I remembered some words about hope and resurrection, but in the immediacy of our grief the words had little comfort. This talk of reunion is all too much for the future. We had seldom been away from Laura in her almost-nine years, and suddenly she was gone. What we wanted most was to be with her then. But she was beyond our reach, and our grief was because of that. In faith, tears are not the sign of despair; we did not weep as those who had no hope. We wept because the end of a day had come, and a savored season had passed.

The suffocating, initial grief eventually began to subside, not because we cared less, but because of the physical and psychic nature of the way that we are put together. We were not hungry, but our bodies had to be nurtured. We didn't want to think about or do anything, but our minds had to be engaged. We were bowed down in spirit, and our souls had to have refreshment.

It is at the waning of the shock and unusually intensive grief period that any person faces the most serious test. The fact of death is established in the mind; the supporting arms of friends have subsided, of necessity; and we are alone with our crisis.

Every critical event—death, divorce, job loss, disability, wrong decision, conflict—has this moment in its dynamics: that moment when, after the rush of details and emergency adjustments and after the first shock waves, we are alone with our crisis.

It was at this point that my family discovered, although we never verbalized it this way, that the only viable way to overcome tragedy and disappointment is by a redefinition of existence in light of what has transpired, a redefinition that has to be made with each experience that causes us to remember the crisis.

Redefinition can be made in a general sense; that is, we can decide that redefinition will be our mode of coping, but each new experience will challenge our commitment to this course. What is redefined is our life after the event. We cannot redefine the event itself. The death has happened; it cannot be redefined. The divorce event has been completed; it cannot be redefined. The job has been lost; it cannot be redefined. The unfortunate decision has been made; it cannot be redefined. The crisis, whatever it is, cannot be redefined. It is only the post-event existence that is subject to redefinition.

The sad alternatives to redefinition are either a melancholy kind of existence or a stoical detachment from life. The person who feeds upon the crisis, but never takes individual responsibility for one's activity after the crisis has happened, begins to deposit neuroses in the personality. All of us have pockets of neuroses in our makeups and all of us have the residue of neurotic reactions, but there is no health in allowing a crisis to fix our reactions to the rest of life. To be sure, death or any of these other events changes the way we look at realities around us, for life can never, never be the same. This is natural. It need not be pathological.

Some time after Laura's death I returned to St. Joseph's

Hospital to visit a child. As I made my way up the stairs and into the pediatric ward I realized that I was all too close to those frightful moments of the previous summer. The tendency toward the neurotic in me suggested that I should turn around and not attempt to go on. Perhaps that is what I should have done. But the danger was that on the strength of this reaction I would have made other unhealthy decisions. Knowing in a moment that that would be a fruitless direction, I went on. I haven't had to go there since, but to some degree, every hospital stimulates my memory, and I know that the healthy choice is to side with the reality of what is happening now. You see, when I entered that corridor I relived a terrible moment, but the present moment was a different one, and that was the moment upon which I had to base my response.

To refuse to redefine our existence after tragedy will hamper our relationships at home and at work and will render our lives dull and unexciting, staid and uneventful, decadent and unadventurous.

Equally perilous is the denial reaction to a crisis. Instead of facing what has happened or even feeding upon it, we decide that it really didn't happen, and we live in that nebulous world where there is no contact with reality. We do not admit to living in a world that is post-tragedy, but in a contrived world that supposes to be pre-tragedy. And we do have to do a lot of contriving when we deny death, or separation, or disappointment; but it is an unstable world in our minds, and it carries with it no joy.

The healthy response is to redefine life after a crisis, for to redefine is to style one's life on the basis of a reality that can be grasped. In my experience this redefinition involves two essential ingredients—memory and expectation.

The process of redefinition begins when the event comes to consciousness. Whatever the crisis is, we know that there are countless stimuli that remind us of it. It is at this point that memory does its work. It may be painful; it may be joyful; but either way, memory is essential if we are going to reshape our lives after tragedy.

20

If it is a painful memory, then we are to endure it with our whole soul and body. I know that awful memories carry with them a physical sensation that is as real as an assault and that the painful memory is borne as one would bear a brutal blow to the body. It is not to be denied or fed upon, but acknowledged and sustained. Poet William Henley's stanza in "Invictus" is a model for this kind of defiant endurance:

> In the fell clutch of circumstance
> I have not winced nor cried aloud.
> Under the bludgeonings of chance
> My head is bloody, but unbowed.[3]

If the pain is because of one's own sin, then the work of memory is much more difficult because guilt begins to complicate the ability to redefine life. It is easy for an outsider to say that we have to overcome our guilt. But it is true. The person who can find no resolution in seeking God's forgiveness needs some professional help to uncover the source of the immobilization that keeps one from working through painful memories of a critical experience. This might take a long time, but it is the right road to health.

Alongside painful memories, there are joyful memories that we have to treasure. When a joyful experience comes to consciousness, I have learned to offer praise for it and to exult in it as I would in the warmth of the sun on an early September afternoon or the refreshment of an April shower. One of my most enjoyable recollections of Laura is how, during our popcorn time on Sunday nights, she would finish her bowl of popcorn and then come and sit by me and help me eat mine. When I remember that, I am inexpressibly grateful for it.

Even these pleasurable memories bring with them an intense pain, for we realize that we are looking back upon experiences that are forever gone. This realization, however, must not be allowed to dominate. The important thing is to give praise for the memory just as we would celebrate the beauty of a summer flower or a December snowfall.

We acknowledge memories; we cannot live on them.

The second ingredient of redefinition is expectation. There is, as the poet said, a hope that springs eternal. It is an unexplainable experience of transcendence. I saw it at work in my colleague, Dr. Claypool, during his daughter Laura Lue's months of suffering, when with each recession of hurt his hopes soared like the eagle. I experienced it with each word of continued survival during my daughter Laura's three days in the hospital, though her condition was critical. I saw it recently as a family received from the doctor a few words about an injured loved one's condition. To those detached from the crisis, these prognoses, these slight changes in condition, these vestiges of life seem insignificant compared to the overall crisis. But to those most intimately involved, they are the occasion for a hope that springs eternal.

Besides this kind of hope there is also an expectation at which we have to work, and what a difficult piece of work it is. However difficult it is to envision the future, we do look ahead in expectation, just as we look back in memory. Yet, if the road to memory is fraught with neurotic and psychotic dangers, the path to expectation is doubly perilous. Expectation can become wishful fantasy or even an unhealthy projection. In this work of hoping, we are bent unthinkingly toward passing along conclusions that have been passed along to us, and that kind of work is ineffectual. This does not discount the beauty and the value of the hopeful word which another speaks to us, but this dimension of hope cannot be vicarious. It will be my hope as I work at it, for although hope is given, it also is made.

In my experience, memory and expectation are a part of the same package: I hope because I can remember. To presume on hope is to desecrate memory. To speak of it too soon is to be cavalier about the awful separation of death. If we are not to grieve because of a resurrection-hope, then this human existence is not to be taken seriously. On the other hand, if there is no hope beyond the flesh, then despair will become our rightful companion. I fully expect that the life I remember but cannot now touch is continuing, that the personality I remember but cannot now communicate with is developing. I am not clear on what our future together will be. My strongest vision (and this is about the best I can do at this point in my pilgrimage) is that someday she will introduce me to the Mystery. It is my firm belief that the Word by which God made everything that was made is also the Word that receives us when we leave this body. I do not know why God has chosen to use human flesh as the womb out of which human personality is born. I do not understand how that personality transcends the body that houses it, but it does. I certainly do not know where that spirit goes when the body can no longer function, but I cannot find any ultimate purpose if that spirit either is dissipated into nonexistence or destroyed with the body.

With the witness of the New Testament, the testimony of reasoning persons through the ages, and the validity of my own memory, I am working out my expectation.

With the interplay of these dynamics—memory and expectation—my family and I are redefining what it means to live after a crisis. Redefinition looks back in memory and ahead in expectation. The transcendence in Laura's life—her spirit that laughed and loved—gives some solid reality to our hope, and we shape the present in light of what we say to our memories and in light of our limited anticipations.

My children are of immense help in this kind of living. A few days after Laura's death, Faye, my daughters, and I were talking in a bedroom upstairs. The doorbell rang. Teresa looked out the window and turned and said, "It's Laura's bike out front." Before I could reassure her that it was not Laura's bike, she and Jennifer were down the stairs and opening the front door. Though my rationality told me what was real in that moment, I, too, experienced a strange expectation.

The children have an unequaled ability to remember with joy, to look ahead in expectation, and to move on with the life that has to be lived now. Without knowing it, they are masters of redefinition. Perhaps this is why Jesus told the disciples that if they wanted to see the kingdom of God they should look at the children. The redefinition of life as we have talked about it is the subject of John 1. To redefine is to believe. To believe is to take up one's son-daughtership (vv. 7, 12-13). To redefine is to see God's Word as the source of all that is (vv. 1-4). To redefine is to live creatively in the tension of the coexistent darkness and light (v. 5). The light shines in the darkness and the darkness has not put it out, neither has the light completely dispelled the darkness. They are side by side, and it is our task to witness to the Light that has come (v. 8). We are not that Light, else we could redefine the crisis; but like John the Baptist, though not the Light, we can have a strong witness to it.

"Let's put a top on the sandbox, Daddy," she said, "so that what we have made won't get torn down." "No," I told her, "that's not the way it is with sandboxes. You create what you can while you're playing; then, if it is destroyed, you start over again."[4]

Every-Person and Hope

It had been ten years since his little girl died, and today Every-Person would visit her grave at the Lonely Place, not knowing that he would be visited by four others. Joining him on this day would be Sadness, Memory, Wishful, and Hope.

Every-Person pulled grass from around the stone that bears her name and brief years, placing the season's flowers where years ago he had laid his heart. As he stood there, Sadness joined him. They clasped hands, standing in silence, save October's gentle wind rustling Autumn's leaves. Together they dropped today's fresh tears. Poetry formed in the mind.[5]

Were she with me this autumn,
we would catch leaves in descent from some tall tree.
I would revel in her laughter,
would embrace her, and she, me.
We would look, as in spring and summer,
for some wooded path
where nature's secrets hide, a place for walking
and if some wonder asked it, for talking.

While we're apart, in worlds now paired;
You there, I in the one we shared;
I muse the passed and passing hours,
Sauntering paths yesterday ours,
As once we did, as did we sing,
In the prismatic hues of spring
As Earth her canvas paints again,
And in the velvet summer rain.

O, the reach that touches nothing
O, the word that is not heard

O, the ear that strains to hear what is not there
and the eye that peers into the dark for a form departed.
O, to speak some loving word
and hear familiar ones in return.
O, to reach for, and find.

Memory tugged at Every-Person's coat bidding, "Come with me." Leaving Sadness there at the grave, he took Memory by the hand. She led him to Former House—the last one Every-Person and his family had lived in together, not far from the cemetery.

Turning the last corner, Every-Person saw Former House; his heart leaped with anticipation. In his excitement he ran on ahead of Memory into the yard and up the porch steps to the front door. He placed his trembling hands on the doorknob, turning it expectantly, but the door would not open. He gripped tighter, trying again, and again, but the door was unyielding.

By this time, Memory had caught up with him. He turned almost innocently to her and cried, "The door, the door, it won't open. Do you have the key?" Shaking her head slowly and touching him on the shoulder, she replied, "No, I don't have the key. You can't get back into Already Gone. All you can do is press against the door, and listen to what was but cannot now be reached. You cannot go in. I brought you here so that you could listen in."

Every-Person pressed hard against the door. A restrained smile replaced the furrow on his brow. Inside, a whole family was eating dinner. He heard table sounds. There were conversations, and laughter—a mother, a father, a preschooler, a second grader, a fourth grader. The voices were painfully recognizable, but he couldn't decipher what they were saying. He could see images inside, but they appeared as a shadowy configuration. He couldn't distinguish any one figure. If only he could catch someone's eye.

His shoulder straining, Every-Person pressed harder against

the door, again turning the knob, pleading with Memory, "Please, can't I go in this one time? It's been ten years. We are so close. I can hear the voices, but I can't tell what they are saying. Please, can't you let me in?" Memory replied sympathetically, "I brought you here to listen in; it's the best I can do." As Memory took him by the hand, Every-Person turned from the door of Already Gone, paused, his eyes shifting as if someone had called out to him, and then, without looking back, walked slowly but unflinchingly away, with Memory beside him. Sadness rejoined them.

As the three walked, Wishful met them in the way. "I am Wishful," she said to Every-Person, "Come with me." Accepting her invitation, he left Memory and Sadness and went with Wishful who took him to the Great Veil that separates the Now from the Not-Yet. "See," she said, "here is the Great Veil. Beyond it lies what you long for with all your heart. Beyond it is the Not-Yet. Let's try to get through."

With Wishful urging him on, he pushed his hands against the Veil, looking for an entry way. Remembering a science-fiction story in which a man found an opening in time and slipped through, but not finding an opening right away, he became obsessed, almost frantic. He ran up and down the Veil, Wishful at his side, but it was no use. He could not penetrate the barrier that holds the secret of the Not-Yet.

He turned to speak with Wishful, but she had slipped away, and in her place stood Hope, right behind him. Recognizing her, he told her that he and Wishful had been up and down the Veil as far as they could travel. They had reached as high as they could, attempting to find an opening, but had failed. Hope looked directly into his eyes, "There is an opening for each person, but you cannot find it by seeking it. In season it will be shown to you."

Perceiving that Hope was wise and strong, he urged her to take him beyond, just for a brief visit. Shaking her head, she replied, with pity in her speech, "No, I can't do that." Believing her and remembering how he had attempted to penetrate the Veil, he pleaded, "Well, then, you have the Force with you, tell me what is over there. If you can't take me through, at least tell me how it is with my little girl." To this tender plea, Hope whispered the most incredible news: "I have never been beyond the Great Veil. I have never been to or seen the Not-Yet. I do my work on this side."

Incredulous at these words, Every-Person stared at her in amazement and disbelief. He stood silently beside her for a little while on the Now side of the Great Veil. Hope broke the silence, "Come, you have learned the lesson at the Veil; let us go." Despite the almost overwhelming pain of disappointment, he turned resolutely, and with Hope beside him, made his way along the path, away from the Great Veil.

As Every-Person and Hope walked the path they came to a flower garden. Hope looked at him, took him by the arm, and suggested softly, "Let's stop in the garden for a little while." And so they did. The garden was past its morning prime; the early refraction of the rising sun and the dew were gone, but the beauty held.

Hope, obviously experienced in garden ways, had a comment to make about almost every flower, including how to cultivate and prune the rarest. She also knew legends about some of the plants of the garden. She told one such story as she stopped beside what appeared to be a morning glory.

"This is the moonflower," she said. "Legend has it that the mother of gardens walked one day among her flowers and plants, conversing with them, touching the dew-laden morning glory, sniffing the primrose, gazing at the variegated beauty of the marigold bed, and taking in the wonder of her creation. As she drank fully of the garden's elixir, she paused, her eyes betraying a brooding, her face a perplexity. 'My garden is graced in the morning as the morning glory opens to the sun; what I need is a lovely flower that can open to the night.' Then her eyes began to play, as if in response to some inner burst of energy; she smiled, bent down and plucked a morning glory from a cluster. Holding it to her breast, she told the flower that she was going to make it into a blossom to grace her evening garden. 'From now on while my other flowers celebrate the sun, you, among all my flowers, will open yourself to the dark and show your glory in the night.' "[6]

With that, Every-Person and Hope left the garden, soon catching up with Wishful, Memory, and Sadness. Every-Person invited them to his house for cheese and hot cider. "It is late," he said, "much too late for travel. See the sun is already behind the hill. There, caught in the lengthening shadow, is my house. The coals are red on the hearth, waiting for fresh logs. Come to my house. We'll pull our chairs to the fire, and I'll read some poetry and the Psalms."

All agreed, and after supper, as he had promised, he took the Bible and a collection of poetry from the shelf beside the fireplace. After reading some psalms, he turned to Robert Frost's poetry and read "Stopping by Woods on a Snowy Evening" and "The Road Not Taken" and other poems.

Then he turned to a little-known piece, Frost's "A Question." He wanted to stir a serious conversation about the meaning of life. He read:

> A voice said, Look me in the stars
> And tell me truly, men of earth,
> If all the soul-and-body scars
> Were not too much to pay for birth.[7]

Then Every-Person laid the book on his lap and asked his guests if Frost were right. Sadness spoke first. "Frost is right. Life is heavy, a vale of tears. The deeper we plumb its depths the more we cry with MacLeish's J.B., 'It's too dark to see,'[8] and agree with the existentialist, 'The meaning is . . . there is no meaning.' "

Memory nodded, half approvingly, but said nothing. But Wishful demurred. "No, no," she said, "Life is a playhouse, and with its toys we create our own little world. Life is—well, it's fantastic."

To this hedonistic thought Memory responded acridly, "You should have been with me when Socrates asked serenely for the hemlock, saying, 'The voice of fate calls. . . .' You should have seen the face of Crito and heard the pathos in his voice when he pleaded with his teacher, '. . . the sun is still upon the hill-tops. . . .'[9] You should have been with me at Golgotha when the Romans executed the Messiah. You should have walked beside me at Auschwitz."

Wishful, impatient with the morbidity of Memory's recollections, put her off as an incurable fatalist. "If you would learn how to forget all of those horrible events you would see that there is in this world much more pleasure than pain," she said. "Those things just happen, and there's nothing to do about them but to enjoy life while you can. Think positively, and everything will turn out as you wish."

Sadness spoke again. "The skeptics are the ones who understand reality. They take seriously the fact of tragedy and absurdity. They are the ones who accept the evidence of Camus's stranger when he accused that from above there is nothing but benign indifference, and Hemingway's Anselmo who held that God is not around here anymore."

Hope listened and pondered what Sadness and Wishful had said, but she had other opinions. "I don't relish disagreement with a sister—Wishful and I are nearly identical twins, you know, but she is wrong. Life is much heavier and more elusive than Wishful will ever admit. Sadness is not far from the truth. The meaning is, there is no meaning . . . that is, if one aspires to know the hidden ontology. So much of life seems meaningless. I could name a hundred instances, but," and with this conjunction Hope broke into poetry:

> I believe, in the absence of proof
> That our groanings
>   the core of all existence perturb
> And are heard.
> That someday an eonian silence
>   will be broken,
> Making understandable the absurd.

Copyright ©1984 by G. Temp Sparkman.

After additional dialogue, Every-Person poked the logs. The group turned from its ponderous discussion to eat cheese, sip hot cider, and count the sparks rising from the dying fire. It was altogether a sacred moment—an Emmaus Road experience—the existential and the transcendent meeting in the humanplace and embracing one another. "Come," said the host, "the guest rooms are ready. You must rest for tomorrow's journeys."

As the new day dawned, the guests were eager to be on their way. Sadness was up first. Every-Person saw her to the door, thanking her for standing beside him at the Lonely Place. They spoke with tears, and she was on her way.

No sooner had Sadness left than Memory appeared at the door. Every-Person thanked her for taking him back to Former House where his family had known life together. Memory stood for a moment, looking at him with compassion, remembering how longingly he had wanted to reenter that house. She could still see him pressing against the door of Already Gone. She put her hands around his hands, raised them to her chin, and said, "I wish I could have done more." With that, Memory walked away.

As Every-Person stood, pondering what Memory had done for him, Wishful bounded into the room, approaching him at the door. He embraced her. "Wishful, I love you," he said, "You came to me in the pain of Memory's company, and tried to help me get beyond the Great Veil. I'll never forget how you ran its length with me, how you tried to help me find an opening." Wishful giggled, kissed him on the brow, and skipped away.

Then came Hope. "Can't you stay longer?" Every-Person asked, "Must you be on your way so soon? You taught me the primeval lesson at the Great Veil. Let's talk about that. Stay for breakfast and the morning. You can be away by noon. Please, can't you tarry awhile? Sadness, Memory, and Wishful have already gone. Stay a little longer."

Hope put her hands on Every-Person's shoulders, telling

him, "I must go. Remember what I told you—I do my work on this side of the Not-Yet. Have you not read, '. . . Now hope that is seen is not hope. For who hopes for what he sees? But if we hope for what we do not see, we wait for it with patience' (Romans 8:24-25). The reality of this, of every moment, is made up of both what appears to be and what is beyond appearance. Thus what appears to be is not wholly what is. Further, that aspect of reality, which is beyond appearance, also in fact, includes what one hopes. Therefore, the reality that is beyond appearance exists in the experience of hoping. And because hope is more than wishful anticipation, then it is a part of the moment of reality which cannot be described by what appears to be."

Then Hope made this pledge, "I promise you that every time Sadness, Memory, and Wishful visit you, I'll come, too. I'll sit with you by the fire. We'll read Frost, and together we'll sing from the psalter: 'The LORD is good; his mercy is everlasting; and his truth endureth to all generations' " (Psalm 100:5, KJV).[10] Amen.

God in Our Joys and Woes

Almost all of us, soon or late, will stand, on some heavy day in life, in a hospital room where someone we love is dying, too soon, and we will hear or perhaps say to ourselves that familiar passage:

> And we know that all things work together for good to them that love God, to them who are the called according to his purpose (Romans 8:28, KJV).

But deep within we will feel that the verse now has an edge on it and does not represent fully what we are feeling. So we will do as many persons have done over and over. We will pick up the Word and read the entire eighth chapter of Romans, and we will ponder with all of our powers of reason and feeling the meaning of this chapter when it is set against death and other crises.

In my youth I understood this verse to mean that life would be one unbroken succession of good will, that there would be a kind of automatic blessing upon me, pushing back evil and failure and leading to unqualified fulfillment. The garden path promised forever to be graced by the sweet fragrance of the rose and the path strewn with its petals. Whether the meaning of the verse was taught that way or I simply heard it that way, I am not sure. But it doesn't matter; I believed all would go well for me, for I loved God and tried diligently to submit to God's purpose for me.

To be sure, there have been moments of highest joy. I have stood at altar with bride, carried three infant daughters from the hospital nursery, been loved by family, been esteemed by a congregation, thrilled to the competition of the "game," known nature in the sense with which Rupert Brooke wrote,

Dawn was theirs, and sunset, and the colours of the earth.[11]

But not all has gone well. Good has not been automatic. The path has been laden with thorns and there have been odors other than the sweet smell of rose. There have been great disappointments as dreams have been crushed. There have been failures in spite of valiant attempts. There have been misunderstandings and alienation. There has been death, and on one early Thursday morning my dear wife and I walked from a Louisville hospital, leaving behind our daughter, Laura, who had just died. Many times since that crushing day, I have asked with Gordon Lightfoot, "Does anyone know where the love of God goes when the waves turn the minutes to hours?"[12]

These adverse experiences have made me ask again: Do all things work together for good to them who love God and are called according to his purpose? I have had to answer no. I have loved God and been obedient to a divine calling, and yet good has not been the only fruit of my experience. Not all has worked as I had hoped or planned. The hard lessons of life have been taught me, and this Scripture from my youth has at times had a hollow ring to it. Then one day I read the same popular Bible verse (Romans 8:28) in the Revised Standard Version:

> We know that in everything God works for good with those who love him, who are called according to his purpose.

Later I saw the J.B. Phillips translation:

> Moreover we know that to those who love God, who are called according to his plan, everything that happens fits into a pattern for good.

Actually the Scripture passage in these later translations is saying the same thing as in the older version, but the various wordings place different accents on the interpretation. In one case it sounds as if everything will work out automatically for good. In the other, it is clear that the meaning is that regardless of what fortunes come to us in this life, God will be with us, helping us through, and further, that out of working through these crises there will also come something positive and instructive, something that will, as one writer has said, "Give weight and depth and gravity and make it (life) extraordinary, rapturous, magical, and real."

I have seen over and over how the worst of circumstances has produced good. Don't misunderstand me, as I perhaps misunderstood those who taught me, to mean that I have been delivered from the circumstances. No, the promise is not that we will be delivered from, but that we will overcome. The experiences of pain will not go away, but they will be worked through, and out of them, something good and positive will come.

I have some friends who know this truth. Recently my colleague in religious education at Midwestern Baptist Theological Seminary faced the prospect of death within a very short time. He did not face it as a ". . . quarry-slave at night, scourged to his dungeon,"[13] but with a certainty that the God of life was also the God in death, and that in the journey into the unknown there would be a central wisdom to guide the way. Though delivered from death, he was not exempted from suffering. From the suffering came a new perspective on his earthly existence.

In the summer of 1968 the eight-year-old daughter of my pastor at the Crescent Hill Baptist Church in Louisville was diagnosed as having leukemia. In his first sermon after receiving that dreadful news, John Claypool recounted George Buttrick's hope-filled words about the Dead Sea. Rather than contrast the Dead Sea with the Sea of Galilee—one salty and not capable of supporting life; the other, fresh and life supporting—Buttrick finds another dimension in the Dead Sea. He says that while it is true that the sea is a dead end for the flow of water, there is still an outlet. The waters stop their downward spill in this salty pool, but there is an upward outlet. As the salt water responds to the heat of the sun a residue of potash is left along the rim of the sea. Buttrick claims that engineers have estimated that there is enough potash there to fertilize the entire earth for at least five years.

John Claypool concluded his sermon:

When no outlet is open except surrender to the sky in helplessness, even this response is not without its positive residue, for out of it can come the miracle of new life. So this is my intention: I will do all I can; stay open and hopeful at every point, and finally surrender my burden to the sky. And surely, surely, out of that, some form of life, even if it is just potash, will mark the spot and something good will remain to show for it.[14]

His daughter died in January 1970. She had not been spared early death, and the family had not been spared the painful agony of watching her suffer or, finally, of giving her up. But as awful as it was, the family survived the ordeal of suffering, the shock of death, and the gnawing pains of separation; for God worked with them. By being honest and open, John Claypool saw his hope fulfilled, for something good did remain to show for it. The cynic is wrong. Our appeals to the sky are not met with benign indifference, but with healing empathy.

In spite of the cataract of woe, nothing can separate us from God—neither death, powers, principalities, the present, the future, height, nor depth. No politic, no time dimension, no spatial measure can come between us. Though there will be times when God will seem very far away, we can be assured that we will not be left to the wreckage of fate. Problems, setbacks, difficulties, and tragedies will not bring us to ruin. God will be with us, and from the ruins we will salvage our last vestige of energy and move on to make existence creative. We can take courage in God's word to Moses: "Go tell the children of Israel that I hear their groanings" (see Exodus 3:16-17), and Jesus' words, "I am come that you might have life; that your joy might be full" (see John 10:10 and 16:24).

But God also is with us in our joys, helping us to be fully present to them. Richard Bach's Jonathan Livingston Seagull knew such moments of pleasure when sailing the highest skies. With the risk of every daring maneuver he found a new joy and exulted fully in what he had learned. "How much more there is now to living," he said to himself from heights the ordinary gulls held no dreams of.[15]

There are many persons around us who cannot really celebrate the good in this life. As children in school caught having fun when there is so much work to be done, these overzealous folks apologize for their defection. With the efficiency of Western compartmentalizing of existence, they regulate their pleasure with the same stringency as their work. In miserliness they play Scrooge to their emotions, managing them so carefully that one wonders if ever they laugh with abandon, resonating with the wonders and joys of this life.

After Homer's Ulysses had returned Chryse's daughter, who had been held captive by the Sons of Atreus, the whole company made sacrifice to Apollo, eating to full satisfaction and passing the drinking bowl among them. Of the oblation, Homer wrote: "Thus all day long the young men worshipped the god with song, hymning him and chaunting the joyous paean, and the god took pleasure in their voices. . . ."[16]

Religious humankind has not found it easy to admit that singing and dancing delights the God who made us and that God joins us in the celebration. Surely the God who, surveying the horizons of creation, expressed unbounded pleasure, also listens in on our merriment and says of it, "That is good; I will be joyful, too."

The joy in which God joins us is not along the yellow-brick road or in the concourse of the fabricated reality of the amusement park. Rather, it is grounded in the integrity of the good itself. It issues from being as fully human as we can be, from being present to existence as it comes to us or as we go to meet it. It is, in fact, set in contrast to the absurdities of life, for God truly works with us for good; God is on our side.

This working for good, which God and we are about, is within the context of God's purpose. The ultimate intent is not apparent to us transient creatures, and however devotedly we focus on understanding it, we come away with only partial particularizations. In spite of such limitation, we can at least suggest that God working in us for good implies some cosmic, some individual purpose, that creation is intended to be more than the chaos which is evident to the observer, that human personality is made for an essential integrity—to conform to the image of the Christ—that we were not meant to be divided in our social relations or in our inner being.

In the end then, what can be said of the pledge that God will work in us for good in all things? At least this: In this life there will be times of unabated pursuit of dreams when our verve is as the lion's and when our spirits will soar as the eagle's to lofty heights. There will be times when we can barely muster the strength to stand and we will swallow our hymns of praise. There will be times when we will say with John Cardinal Newman, "The night is dark, and I am far from home."[17] There will be times of failure, disappointment, frustration, conflict, and death.

However, we need not despair at such a mixed existence, for in it God will work for good, will help us reshape our lives in light of events. God will help us celebrate the joys that are before us and bear the woes that come upon us. Our Maker is on our side, and when "waves turn the minutes to hours," we will know where the love of God is. It is with us.[18]

In Response to Absurdity

Have not we all wondered with that extraordinary poet William Shakespeare,

> Whether 'tis nobler in the mind to suffer
> The slings and arrows of outrageous fortune,
> Or to take arms against a sea of troubles,
> And by opposing end them. To die: to sleep;
> No more; And by a sleep to say we end
> The heart-ache, and the thousand natural shocks
> That flesh is heir to. . . .[19]

and whether life "is a tale told by an idiot, full of sound and fury, signifying nothing."[20]

When I ponder the "outrageous fortunes" of this life—disease, suffering, death, relational problems, misunderstandings, separations, the abuse of power, the demeaning of human dignity—I am drawn to beating my breasts and crying, "Yes, good poet, there are times when I feel that existence signifies nothing."

At other times the unbounded joys of this life—the color of the seasons, the affirming friend, the unsolicited kiss of a child, the challenge of a worthy task—make me glad to be alive and willing to pay the price of this terrestrial experience.

It is easy to answer Shakespeare's charge too quickly and automatically, either from despair or from an unthinking stance that purports to be Christian. The pitiful victims of our society will answer, "Yes, life is too exacting." The mother of ten children in the ghetto, whose husband has abandoned her and whose system works against rather than for her, can justly say, "Yes." The huddled refugees of this world can, with cause, answer, "Yes." Sometimes these answers given by the grieving and the desperate seem strange to persons who have not known suffering. How easily we tire of others' grief and pain. Nonetheless, they are legitimate, human responses to life's misfortunes.

On other occasions, the Christian is often tempted to answer hastily and say, "No." Nothing invalidates Christian hope like giving premature answers to life's deep questions before one wrestles with these questions. Such unthoughtful answers deny the evidences of human frailty and suffering and raise grave questions about the substance of faith. If one must say, "No, the price for birth is not too great," without experiencing the full pain of that price, then faith is mere verbalism and not genuine experience.

In either case, the automatic answer is insufficient—the yes from despair, the no from pseudo-faith—because the response, if it is to be valid, must come from the struggle.

The woes of existence that test us come to us as absurdities, and absurdities they are. When I was young, our brother and sister Jews in Europe were herded, clothed only in their faith, into gas showers and killed. Can anyone even fathom, let alone give a rational explanation for, the demonic at Auschwitz? In that same historical drama, a Christian nation dropped atomic bombs on Japanese people. Can anyone give a rational explanation for the moral breakdown demonstrated at Hiroshima? In the Vietnam action, napalm burned the bodies of innocent children. Can anyone give a rational explanation for this hell within a hell? Earth lives with the threat of destruction in nuclear war. Can this madness even be imagined?

In 1970 in my church in Louisville, two little girls died of leukemia. Can anyone tell me why? In March of this year a friend of my daughter died at thirteen, mercifully delivered from a devastating disease. Beyond naming the disease and tracing its rapid spread, can anyone give a rational explanation of such an incredible terror? I doubt it. The absurd defies reason.

Still the absurd is before us, and we stand in its wake sometimes with inquiring eyes asking what happened, sometimes slumping, simply acquiescing to its blows, sometimes musing, trying to put its devastation into some rational, manageable form.

We are not the first to walk in absurdity's darkness, to look, to strain for light, to attempt to find some reasonable explanation for irrationality, to seek order in the chaos, to search for some comfort from pain. In the ancient and beautiful *The Epic of Gilgamesh*, the hero said at the death of his friend, Enkidu, "An evil fate has robbed me."[21] Humanity has, through the ages, believed what Utnapishtim said to Gilgamesh, "When the Annunaki, the judges, come together, and Mammetun, the mother of destinies, together they decree the fates of men."[22]

Is that the answer? Do some higher beings—or even one— manipulate us as puppets, causing us to rise and suddenly to fall, to be animated, to lie in silence, and finally or early to be destroyed?

Job did not think so. He faced absurdity, but he would not name its author Fate. "The LORD gave, and the LORD has taken away; blessed be the name of the LORD" (Job 1:21), is what he said. In the play *J.B.*, by Archibald MacLeish, Eliphaz suggests to Job, "Our guilt is underneath the Sybil's Stone: not known."[23] Job reacts—violently, the stage direction says. "Can we be men and make an irresponsible ignorance responsible for everything? I will not listen to you."[24]

Yet what difference does it make? Who was right, Gilgamesh or Job? Ancient answers do not deliver us from the struggle. We are caught in our own existential plight, unsure of when to say, "Blessed be the name of the Lord," or "It was God's will." To admit to the opposites of these assertions is to border on insurrection or at least to admit to powers greater than God's. Will a man say, "God be cursed," or admit that a greater will than God's has caused this thing?

For my part I will not curse, nor can I limit, God's power. Still I have my questions—hard questions without answers— and living with these hard questions, I have come to expect no answer—at least just now. Like Gilgamesh, I have found that no one will "assemble the gods" to draft an answer to my queries.

What then is one to do? Is there a way out? Life has shown at least two paths through the confusion. Briefly put: I can give myself to whatever human dimensions figure into the absurdities, for example, in the face of the unexplainables of war, I can work for peace. Second, when there is no way to touch the absurdity, as in death, I can live with creative and resolute hope.

As to the accessible absurdities, they come as a drama without ending lines, without the actors' finale and bows; a drama with a beginning, but seemingly no end. However, the actors change, and as ordained by the Creator, we have a stake in the plot and a contribution to make in writing the script; for we have been made as responsible persons in spite of the fact that we have so often forfeited.

The irrational will always be out there against order and sanity, beyond our explanation or control, acting on us. But we are not obliged to acquiesce helplessly to it. We can and should raise our protest. Bombings and terrorism have human origins and can be stopped. The obscenity of poverty has a remedy. Human degradation can be relieved. The abuse of power can be corrected.

Just before mesmerizing the nation with a litany of dreams in his famous "I Have a Dream" speech, Martin Luther King, Jr., told his suffering followers, "Go back to Mississippi, go back to Alabama, go back to South Carolina, go back to Georgia, go back to Louisiana, go back to the slums and ghettos of our modern cities, knowing that somehow this situation can and will be changed."[25] Carlyle Marney knew that "in all the turnings of history, God's history has moved toward redemption. The redeemed have been involved in all the turnings of history."[26]

What then of the bewildering absurdities that we cannot touch with our powers? I narrow the circle of possibilities now to the irrational in my own experience. Again, comes truth from *The Epic of Gilgamesh*:

> When he had gone one league the darkness became thick around him, for there was no light, he could see nothing ahead and nothing behind him.

That line is repeated through seven leagues. Then we hear:

> When he had gone eight leagues Gilgamesh gave a great cry, for the darkness was thick and he could see nothing ahead and nothing behind him. After nine leagues he felt the north wind on his face, but the darkness was thick, and there was no light, he could see nothing ahead and nothing behind him. After ten leagues the end was near. After eleven leagues the dawn light appeared. At the end of twelve leagues the sun streamed out.[27]

I have been there, standing in the thickest of darkness, crying out; I have felt the north wind on my face and entered the eleventh league, facing the light of dawn. But I do not yet know the twelfth league where the sun streams out. I know that Light has come into the world, and that it has not been put out. At the same time, how honestly it must be admitted that neither has the darkness dissipated. The light and the dark coexist, but the twelfth league is on the way. That is the promise of the Advent, the surety of the resurrection.

Still, I speak of it with reserve. To claim to have full light when one sees only a glimmer invalidates the hard struggle of the dark days of suffering. It lends little seriousness to this struggling pilgrimage, and it makes the hope we talk about sound ephemeral and without substance. The ready and the superficial word is forever suspect in the face of absurdity.

Two scenes from the film version of Joseph Stein's *Fiddler on the Roof*, a chronicle of Russian Jews before the Russian Revolution, teach the lesson. The first is the incident when the Tsar's soldiers senselessly raid the wedding party of Tevye's daughter. After the fray ends, Tevye stands looking upward with a quizzical expression and with open palms of inquiry. As usual, there is no reply from the heavens—only a deafening silence. Although it seems that there is in the

43

silence no explanation, perhaps there is, in the ultimate sense, an answer of sorts. Against the absurd there may be, however feeble at the time of the impact, an answer, and the answer is: "There is no explanation; but there still is a life before you. Take hold of it and God will be with you."

The other particularly poignant scene is the exodus of Tevye, his family, and his friends from their village. The entire film has focused on calamity and celebration, struggle and resolution. When the final scene comes, the photography is captivating, the choreography is arresting, the music is filled with pathos. As the procession drones down the road away from the village, the viewer reflects on the scope of the film—remembering all that this community has suffered, and because of history, anticipating the enormity of the Holocaust to come. In the midst of this arresting and pathetic scene, Tevye turns, looks backward, and sees the fiddler, playing his bouyant tune and dancing to center stage. Then, Tevye joins him in his creative response to absurdity.

A scene from another drama comes to mind. A teacher, a good man, is finally done in by the religious establishment which his style and speech threatened to undo. He hangs, dying at the hands of the Roman executioner, repeating a psalm and making other utterances audible to those close around him. By any standard of justice this man does not deserve death, but there he hangs. Perhaps the darkening skies are but cosmic sensitivities to the absurdity being perpetrated just outside Jerusalem.

Standing on this side of that historic event, we, of course, know another scene; but had the followers of Jesus known Shakespeare's assertion, what would their response have been? I suspect that they would have agreed with the poet.

To be sure, there is much in our existence that is absurd, and we are feeble to prevent it. However, we do have the power to respond with renewed commitment to whatever in these absurdities is within the range of human solution. Too, we can live in the hope that God's creative energy will continue to surprise us, as it did the women who came to the tomb on Easter morning. Thus can we stand against whatever outrageous fortune meets us in the way.[28]

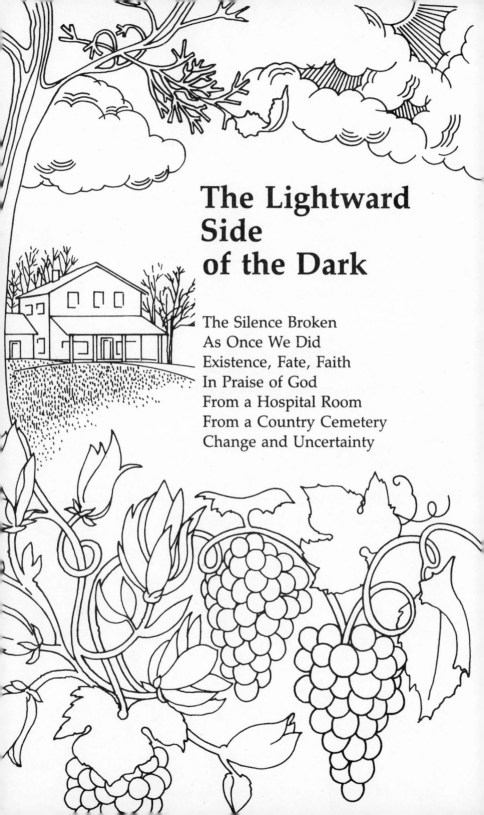

The Lightward Side of the Dark

The Silence Broken
As Once We Did
Existence, Fate, Faith
In Praise of God
From a Hospital Room
From a Country Cemetery
Change and Uncertainty

The Silence Broken

I believe, in the absence of proof,
That our groanings
The core of all existence perturb,
And are heard.
That someday an eonian silence
Will be broken,
Making understandable the absurd.

That in the endless abysmal stretch
An affect moves
From its resident vortex in space
To our place,
In mystical speech, resonating with
Our deepest cries,
Giving the void an empathetic face.

That in ambiguous existence
A center point
Absorbs the onslaught of fate's ill winds,
And withstands.
That suff'ring, querying persons come in their
Ambivalence
To find at bottom the eternal hands.

As Once We Did

While we're apart, in worlds now paired;
You there, I in the one we shared;
I muse the passed and passing hours,
Sauntering paths yesterday ours,
As once we did, as did we sing,
In the prismatic hues of spring
As Earth her canvas paints again,
And in the velvet summer rain.

Existence, Fate, and Faith

Existence comes as gift from God,
A thing possessed in human flesh:
Bone, sinew, tissue, nerve, vein, blood;
An enigmatic, mortal mesh;
An essence by a spirit shown;
A made-one by the Maker known;

A person with the given right
To be, belong, to breathe the air
Of each new day, to walk the night
And feast on vesperal starry fare;
To listen to the sounds of earth
As all creation sings its mirth;

To touch on morning's bloom the dew;
To savor grape fresh from the vine;
Imbibe each season's luscious brew;
To dialogue as by design;
To dream, to fantasize, contrive,
To praise, to curse, to be alive.

My common gift; my common deed:
I am! I am! I do exist.
As it began, my father's seed,
My mother's womb as lovers kissed,
Collaborated; me, conceived,
And birthed the life I but received.

Full-blown existence was conferred.
In infant cry, receiving it,
I took the life that was proffered,
Then breath by breath held on to it.
I am! I am! I do exist.

I am! I am! I do exist.

But on my being, profligate,
Another given comes as cause,
Existence now is joined by Fate.
To human will she gives no pause,
To pleasure cold, to love unknown,
She works her mission, taciturn.

Against Existence, Fate appears.
Though not with destiny the same
She flies on wings of cosmic fear,
Consigning demons' work to shame.
She rides in storms, no victims knows,
Without design, no mercy shows.

Without control she stalks the earth;
Holds no divine apostolate.
Nor bounded she by heav'nly girth.
But keeps the circumstantial date.
Demonic, dreaded, feared, untamed:
Fate, she, by hapless victims, named.

With Joy, the offspring reveling
In Being's house, Fate intervenes.
She stills Joy's feet, bedeviling
Her song; her birthright contravenes.
She leaves in wake a gray malaise;
Contests Existence at the base.

Against Existence, Fate appears,
So Being cannot now beget
Full pleasure, for the pain and tears.
Though stunned, she stands, unshaken yet,
For something at the center holds.
The bottom shakes. The center holds.

The body from the deep draws breath,
As pain, acute, completes its course,
And would send Being to the death,

Except an unrelenting force
Strong from the center emanates,
The smothering psychic shroud abates.

Soft, measured words alone convey
A reticence to postulate.
Once profuse lips are fain to say
What they believe, anticipate;
Nor certainty do they require,
But are inclined more to inquire.

Yet in the asking Faith is born,
For 'tis of mystery Faith inquires,
And does not judge the quest forlorn,
But wonders why when Fate conspires
The Maker does not speak, or seem
To care enough to intervene.

Then counter to our helplessness,
Our birth, Hope renegotiates.
And in the second genesis
The pristine image, she resets;
Awakens too the pow'r to cope,
And Joy returns to dance with Hope.

Though Unfaith too the darkness bears,
Both by the Grand Designer known,
Unfaith and Faith, Fate's blows endure.
But Faith speaks of the dawn foreshown,
Anticipates the coming light
And leads the pilgrim through the night.

In Praise to God

O God within us, but not imprisoned by our finiteness; O God beyond us, but not alien to our human situation, you are the source of all that is praiseworthy, and we praise you.

O creating God, who shaped what is from what was not, we praise you for your creating spirit which moved over the primeval abyss and wrested the light from the pitch black of night.

O renewing God, we praise you for the sun's light which chases the night, giving us a new day; for the drink of November brew which tells us that we are alive.

We praise you for the generational stream in which we live—for the innocence and play of childhood, the dynamism of our days of youth, the productivity of the maturing years, and the wisdom of age.

We praise you, O God of beauty, for this brilliant autumn. We walk its corridors and on every hand are drawn aside by burning bushes, and stand in wonder on holy ground. We put off our shoes and listen for your word of perspective.

We praise you for the touch of artistry that turns common phenomena into images, ordinary words into poetry; that holds together the strings, winds and horns, to make a symphony.

O God of truth and integrity, we praise you for the act of courage that will not forever allow the human spirit to be driven as sand and leaves by the wind, but which lifts us to full measure to declare "We are persons in God's image."

We praise you for the stirrings of peace that move us in

love toward those who move toward us in hate.

We praise you for the strength of conscience to cry out against the waste of war, the evil of power abused, the inhumanity of poverty.

We praise you for the light of reason that frees us from the bonds of superstition, that keeps us from the preys of ignorance; that leads us to love the good and the true.

We praise you for this life, and though it is often as precarious as the flickering candle flame, we live in hope that it will stay the darkness and that ill winds will not snuff it out. Amen.

From a Hospital Room

Outside the hospital window a tiny leaf holds tenaciously to the branch. Already victor over driven rain and snow, it now resists stubbornly the January wind. The other leaves which frolicked in the full bloom of summer have been wrested from the tree, have fallen and been recycled or raked and hauled away.

I don't know how it is this leaf has held, or why, for soon spring buds will push it from its place and to the ground. But there it is, riding the wind, waving, swirling against a blue sky as formerly against the gray, oblivious to its fate.

With eyes still fixed on the clinging leaf my mind turns back inside. I muse—there must be in other rooms here some brave persons holding on, unwilling to give in to the latest wind of adversity. They will not turn loose though their friends of youth have all died and gone. Thus they stand, though prostrate, demonstrating a stubborn will to live.

The musing turns to questioning—is it worth the effort? Then questioning turns to answering. Much there is to answer no, but then who could have seen purpose in a faded, late-clinging leaf? Maybe when our summer is past we may yet speak to life—that it is worth holding to, in spite of pain—and maybe to destiny—that in the inevitable journey into the unknown there will be found a Central Wisdom to guide the way.

From a Country Cemetery

Preston Heights cemetery is on a hill above Quebeck, Tennessee, a mill town begun by some of my ancestors. John Cooper, or Uncle Johnny Cooper as they called him, brought his family here from Belfast, Ireland, around the turn of the century. He built this town around a lumber mill. We called it the "saw mill" and most non-farmers in these parts worked there. I remember how the big lumber trucks, loaded with logs taken from the forests all around, would roar down the gravel-covered road past our house.

My father, James Cooper Sparkman, did not work at the mill. He was not suited by temperament or dream for the mill, for he was a free-spirited man with social interests. He was a salesman for a wholesale grocer, was active in civic affairs, and was what today would be termed a social liberal. He raised money for the widows, sat with the sick, promoted community activities at the Quebeck school, and established this cemetery. He was not a church man. I suspect that he was rejecting the narrow world which the town's religion embraced.

Dad and my mother, Emma, a pretty and witty girl and a woman with an indomitable spirit in the face of adversity, had nine children, five boys and four girls. We lived, loved, struggled, and survived in a white frame house across town but visible from this cemetery hill. Dad was buried here in 1936; Mother in 1942.

After Mother's death the home place had to be sold and those of us who still lived at home left our birthplace. Two of my sisters, Pattie Marie and Fannie Cooper, themselves too young for such responsibility, took Frances Moore and me to Old Hickory where they became parents to us. Except for one brother, the rest of the family was settled somewhere in Tennessee.

Our family has returned to this hill to bury family and friends, and today, Fannie Cooper. The quality of her quiet and unselfish life made it easy for her minister to formulate an appropriate word at the memorial service earlier at Old Hickory where she had worked since she left Quebeck in the 1930s. Today she is back home and the last words are being spoken by a funeral director who has buried all but one of our family members who have died. He speaks today haltingly, and his voice quivers, for he remembers being in our home many times to gather around our lively family table to eat and to laugh with us. He tells the mourners gathered around the grave about his fond memories of these happy occasions.

As I brace against the cold wind up here, I am drawn to the home place on the other hill. I look, and I ponder whether the memories of joy and pain which those walls hold have not broken from their prison of the past and have come over to this hill today to attempt through memory's gift to ease the loneliness of this moment. Perhaps it would be some word from Dad's strong determination, or a line of Mother's wit, or some secret word between brothers and sisters which only they and time know about. Who knows, or who can say? Still it is a time to wonder about the deep mysteries of time and of space, of love and of relationships, of life and of death.

The last words are spoken. Those who could not be at the funeral service a hundred miles away pass by the open casket, an important ritual in the culture of the region. There are embraces and tears. Then the grave is covered and surrounded by the flowers sent from friends of many years. The wind animating the cedars seems to speak the wisdom of Ecclesiastes:

> To every thing there is a season, and a time to every purpose under
> the heaven:
> A time to be born, and a time to die. . . .

Then shall the dust return to the earth as it was:
and the spirit shall return unto God who gave it.
—Ecclesiastes 3:1-2, 12:7, (KJV)

I add, in my own heart, "And the spirit who departs today leaves behind a gentle memory."

Change and Uncertainty

O Ancient of Days, as children at play, we gave little thought to the days of our lives. Caught up in living, we held no interest in the meaning of it all. But as the ground plan dictates, the days turned to years, and the years to decades. With this irresistible and irrevocable advance, we became more reflective, pondering the meaning of existence.

Once so sure that our life energy would never be depleted, we now realize the frailty of our existence. The life we took so for granted, we now treasure for its sheer gift and promise.

Once so confident that every question had an answer, we now stand perplexed in the face of life's riddle. Although, in quantity, we have more answers, the questions are deeper, the mystery intensified.

How full of wonder are we that we can utter, "I am." How humbled are we that the next breath is not guaranteed. We give gratitude, O Ancient of Days, for the years given to us on this earth.

O God of the Not-Yet, who rules over time and eternity, keep alive in us the hope that will help us, in the face of the uncertain, to hold to your promises, to be free to celebrate the day which we can embrace and delight in.

Even when shadows of death enshroud us, we light the Advent candle against the darkness, waiting in faith before its warmth and light.

O Ancient of Days, O God of the Not-Yet, "Our help in ages past, our hope for years to come," be in and with us. Amen.

The Secrets in the Seasons

Markings

Morning and snow
Betray the path of wind
And where rabbits run.

Time and event
Etch telling lines of age
And write on the soul.

All markings bear
Ultimate mysteries;
And mortals wonder.

All bear wisdom,
At bottom seen, felt,
But unutterable.

The End of a Season

The God I am trying to understand and who, without complete understanding, I worship and serve does not thunder audibly in the spheres to disclose an ultimate identity or reveal the purpose toward which existence is moving. Neither does God answer my queries about life and death. Still I can hear the transcendent speech.

God speaks with a natural world so beautiful as to defy description; God speaks when a full moon glimmers over the lake while the winds move the waves gently to the shores. God tells me things through my brothers and sisters, all around.

For my most pressing current need God talks to me most clearly through the cyclic processes of nature's work. There is a morning and a twilight. There is a spring and a winter. There is a blooming and a withering. In this process God is telling me much about life and death.

God tells me that life is to be approached with the freshness of the dawn when the light breaks over the darkness and the birds break into song, that life is to be lived with the creativity of spring when that which to most observers is dead is renewed, when that which is seemingly hopeless is redeemed. God tells me that life is to be celebrated with the immediacy of the blooming of flowers which show themselves for but a brief moment and then withhold their beauty until the creative cycle comes around to flower again.

Besides speaking about life, God in this kind of process tells me much about disappointment, about reversals, about death. What I hear is that everything is subject to a cyclic course, that when it has ended, however prematurely or without reason, it is to be taken as life is taken and with equal grace as the end of a season.

Mass of Beauty

Sometimes it seems significant and alive; at other times it is lackluster and moribund. That's the way my work is.

Take, for instance, yesterday, when God brought out hundreds of glistening, iced vessels for a wintertime Mass of Beauty. I was inside and warm, facing an agenda of committee work and some necessary reading. But in light of what was happening outside, it seemed trivial. My papers felt like weights in my hands, the books dull and without appeal, for after all, a celebration was underway. Since I was made for living, I sensed that life was somewhere else. At other times and on other days it would be different, but yesterday my soul was restless for the beauty beyond the walls.

The God of diversity and balance was on my side, I suspect. Since it was surely the Creator's wish for me to be out for beauty, it was surely by a providential grace that I was able to tend to my necessary work, giving integrity to my commitments, and still join the celebration.

So out I went into the temple of inverted chandeliers, where fluted music sang from an evenly paced, rippling creek and where stringed wind whispered the word of mystery and disclosure, where a small dangling limb prevented my car's passage, challenging me to leave shelter for a full sensual experience.

I was out for beauty and my whole being took in as much as it could hold. The Ultimate Energy is a Great Creator who can hang water on a million trees and move back the winter clouds allowing the sun to make countless diamonds, one of every frozen drop.

One of these days when I am tempted to fence God in with my hopelessness, or with my partially true theology, or with my obscurant cultural situation, I'll remember yesterday's

Mass of Beauty, and I'll celebrate a God who calls us to the ordinary and also away from it to something grander, a God who is too awesome to be seen, a God who is too loving to hide from us.

The January Snow

Autumn brilliance is but a memory; spring green, only an anticipation; and winter's landscape stands frozen, bleak, forsaken. The heavy, auguring sky closes in on the earth, as if to give it further insult by depriving it of light, perhaps even, to cover it with cosmic soot. But, wonder of wonders, from the blackness, white flakes appear, falling gently on the naked limbs and covering the stubby ground. A January snow comes to my little four-season acre of the planet.

The snow carries a peculiar witness to the meaning of gospel which, as the snow, comes as a bright surprise when we are bent under our troubles, a word of acceptance when we are smothered in personal rejection and guilt. Conceptualized in diverse forms, it is the good word that we are children of God, the reassurance that the defection which binds us is neither the essential word about our origin nor the ultimate word about our destiny. It is the word that God accepts us as we are, that Jesus the Christ has incarnated that acceptance, that Second Adam has appeared to set aright the creation which God is about.

In the snow is the lesson of paradox, for it is at once indescribably beautiful and unmercifully treacherous. Too, there is paradox in the word that has been given the church, for it comes both as liberation and demand. It is a given, freeing word; but it cannot hold its essence unless it is fully lived and joyfully shared. Should we think that in hearing the word it becomes ours to keep, or should we think that it can only be proclaimed inside our buildings, or should we think that we can imprison the word within our postulations, we will most surely lose it. If after hearing it we turn in joy to share it, we can most assuredly keep it.

But the demand the word lays on us is not an external

66

imposition. Demand is not an addendum to liberation, not the fine print of an attractive contract. Rather, the call is in the word itself, originating in the joy of having heard the word. Once the word is seen and received, its liberation and demand are simultaneously released. Liberation without boundary is illusory and ultimately insecure; demand without joy is spiritual death. The gospel holds out neither extreme, but comes as paradox.

Unlike the pounding spring storm, the snow is nature's softest voice, coming as a whisper, undetected by the ear, discovered only by the eye or the touch. So, too, the word comes not from the power centers of the world, not from the loud boasts of the ostentatious and the proud, but from the remote region of an empire, from the lips of a Suffering Servant. Therefore, listen intently, for the surprising, paradoxically freeing and demanding word moves quietly, as quietly as the soft snow falls.

It Will Be Green Again

Was the grass really once green, the sounds of birds clearly heard? And did we picnic in the park just six short months ago? Here in the cold winter they seem so far away. The naked trees, the leaden skies seem always to have been, and out ahead for endless time, so that we ask if earth were ever really green, and if the spring will come back again.

Oh yes, the spring will make return. The gray, dull days of cold will pass. The routines now holding us will break. Despair will pass; a reassuring word will come. Presumption that all is lost will be replaced by a shining, fresh expectancy. The future will become a possibility again. The crushing claims on our lives will not forever dominate. In liberation we will learn to choose, and in our choices to be secure.

The sadness weighing down on us will lift, as Joy sounds her call to us. The cause of sadness will not disappear, but Joy will come in spite of it. Then will we laugh again, will dance and sing, will celebrate this life, God's gift to us.

Our draining conflicts will not dissipate. No wind will sweep them fast away. We will go through them and will withstand. Redemption will accrue from our transactions. Relationships will be rescued and restored. Where breaks are too severe for reconciliation, a healing will in time be known.

Was the earth really once green, and will the spring come back again? Oh yes, as sure as ever it were here, as sure as winter is now here, as sure as God exists, the spring, it will return, and the earth be green again.

Spring Green

Spring, in her green, is her own simile. We cannot speak of her as being as green as some other phenomenon, for she is as green as Spring. Thus must other realities beg the simile and hope to be described as being as green as Spring.

In her freshness, however, Spring can be given to the metaphor. This year we sit at her table celebrating her good company, eating heartily of her tasty bread, and drinking her sweet elixir. We walk with her in the early morning, answering her overtures of color and wind with our own lyrics and unscored harmonies. We sit with her at the day's end, applying to the soul's canvas the hues and silhouettes she inspires.

Still, Spring is more. Beyond the simile, which she provides for other of life's realities, and the metaphors, which she generates within human experience, she also uncommonly symbolizes hope and new life. Coming as she does at the end of the frosty winter graced only by intermittent snow and an elegant barren tree on the landscape, Spring defies appearances. The earth, frozen hard underfoot, turns soft and pliable to trowel; unyielding of fruit, turns receptive to seed; without aromatic presence, excites the olfactory sense; colorless, except for the gift of snow, turns yellow and white and lavender, and, of course, green—green as Spring.

We exult in the aroma of Spring, and her color, and we also ruminate. In our hearts we query among our longings and dialogue among our doubts, whether we, like Spring, can also come from the deadness of our winters of broken dreams, our unbelief, our doldrums of cynicism, to new life. In time, we affirm that truly it is so—as the season dead before our eyes is resurrected in full dimension, we too can be restored. We too can be awakened to sensual fulness.

Further, if we ourselves can be renewed within the boundaries of our creaturehood, we can also come alive to a wider hope, a still unformed vision of a season which in her character is, like the green of Spring, without equal.

A Summer Rain

Today the sound of rain on the roof has an uncommon allure, for the land is besieged by drought. I find it irresistible—the urge to go outside and celebrate this scarce summer happening. Once out, I am overtaken by a sense of something Past as well as something Present. The earthy smell of summer rain after drought is not often found in the city. I am taken back to rural origins, where reality wasn't plastic.

But the sense of the Present is what is most real, and I stand before it in consuming silence. I am not alone in my reverence, for the dry, brown grass, now like pine needles to the foot, doffs the falling rain drops, then cradles them as a hen her young. The trees and I dance with the wind, applauding the coming of this summer nourishment.

It is a short fall, hardly enough to send more than a trickle down the spout at the corner of the house. But it is enough to have in it refreshment for a parched earth and a lesson for a resonating human being.

I know the times in my own experience when I am dry of meaning and welcome a life-giving touch, a transforming word. I know, too, the loss of the pungent hour, but also the coming of some inspiring word, some redeeming relationship. I take them in as the grass the rain and clap my hands as the leaves on the tree, for I am weary of drought.

The rain passes, the wind dies, and midsummer Sun reappears in her brightness. The trees drip a few more drops of water to the thirsty grass and stand appealing to the heavens to send more. I wait, too, and appeal for more rain and another drink of life.

Cycles

We mow the grass on summer's yard;
We gather autumn's scraping leaves,
And shovel January's drifted snow
In salutation to decreed,
Unending cycles which we know
To mark our passing years.

We put long hours to noble work;
We frolic in diversive play,
And by recurring schedules ratify
The ancient rhythms that obtain
To circumscribe and verify
Our simple joys and tears.

We live in full our given days;
And in our ending we assume
A quiet posture of repose. In grace
Accepting thus the finitude,
The image which the human face
By ordination bears.

We peer into the dark Not-Yet,
In hope, the unseen we presume,
And, without cynicism's bitter food,
Unfretfully, exuding praise,
Adjudge the teleos as good
Our Maker's work declares.

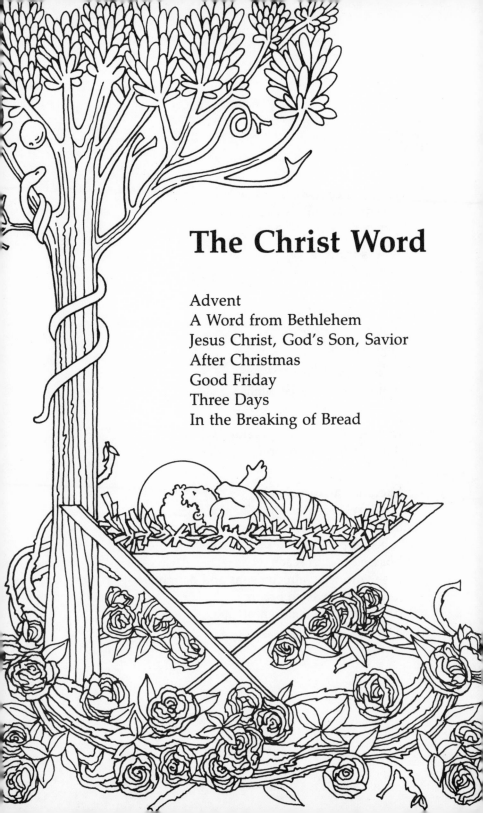

The Christ Word

Advent

There was love here
    but much of lovelessness,
    and he came.

There was truth here,
    but much of error,
    and he came.

There was light here,
    but much of obscurity,
    and he came.

There was God here,
    but much of inaccessibility,
    and he came.

There was sonship and daughtership here,
    but much of alienation,
    and he came.

And because he came:
Love was rekindled in the ashes of anger;
Truth surged in error's den;
Light began pushing back the darkness;
God passed within reach;
And we who were already sons and daughters
    received power to become
    the redeemed children of God.

A Word from Bethlehem

There are three ultimate words about you and me—two of them out of Eden, the third, out of Bethlehem. The first describes us as the Creator intended; the second, as what we have become; and the third, as what we may yet become.

The first word is that upon creating person, God said, "It is good." It is a word of singularity, a word of integrity. The God who made us said of the work, "It fits. The entire design is apposite. Person belongs here in Eden, and both the setting and the form are what I had in mind. And it is good."

Thus were we there, made in the image of God. We did not look like God, or have the power or thought of God. But there we stood, in the image, after the likeness. God looked upon us with no regrets, no plans for changing us, taking us as we were. Liking what was seen, God said, "It is very good."

Accepting us just as we had been made, God was glad in the work. This is always the first word about us. There is a second word, but this is always the first word: God took pleasure in us.

Defection is the second word. Enter the serpent! The God who enjoyed our existence came one day to talk with us, but we were hiding. Something had come between us, and we did not want to see our Maker. The snake had also looked at us, and in slithering about Eden had made his own plans for us. And, oh, the shame. The slimy creature convinced us that the garden was ours alone, that with a significant act of self-assertion we could become as the One who had made us.

Thus we chose to take matters into our own hands on the illusion that we were the complete masters of our destiny. Then thundering through the spheres came the second word about us, and this word was "defection." Before its echoes died, we realized that we had alienated ourselves from the Maker. The second word had been spoken. It was as if the scenario had been orchestrated by demons to seduce our brothers, and sisters as well, and we all forgot who we were.

And God must have wept over it all—God who had formed us out of the dust of the earth and had breathed into us the breath of life and had said, "It is good." But God would not give up so easily, for the grand vision persisted, and beyond the word of our sinfulness, God would speak a third word, and the word would be "reconciliation."

Thus, to Bethlehem. Enter Jesus Christ! Yes, enter, the man! But not in allegory or drama. Jesus Christ entered human history, as real person, true Son. In him the Word, which had brought the worlds into existence, became flesh. He lived before us the true Sonship, not in order to condemn, but to bring us to life.

He judged us, but not with the Law. His judgment was that he lived the true humanity and made us see how we had forsaken the divine intention. He wielded a sword, but its thrust was his own oneness with the Maker, and it exposed our alienation.

Out of Bethlehem, the bidding word is spoken; "the wondrous gift is given." The word is that we have been forgiven, and the gift is the image reawakened. What we could not do on our own, God did in the Christ. Just as the deafening cries of our despair rode the winds in the wilderness, so the radical word of redemption shakes the gates of Eden, and we are welcomed back by a celebrating Maker.

Though home at last, we find that the enticements of the Serpent and the habits of the wilderness are not forgotten. We repeatedly favor them over the impulses of our sonship and daughtership. Thus do we remember Bethlehem so that we might hear the good word again. And still it comes, as always it has, and it tells us that God identifies with us and thus forgives.

My daughter Teresa, just coming of age and going for her driver's license, confessed to the examiner that she was very nervous. She heard in reply that the examiner's own daughter was taking her test across town. As with the examiner, so with God—we tell the plight we are in with our humanity, and God says, "I know. My Son has taken the same test."

The third word is more than a forgiving, restoring word. It is also a call to take up the duties of life in the Garden, to be about the business of the Creator. When we work for a sane balance between the use of the earth's resources and the preservation of the environment, we are on Garden duty. When we work within the ambiguities of the disruptive and disintegrating dynamics of social unrest, we are on Garden duty.

So the word from Bethlehem is sounded and can work healing in the issues of the day—energy, ecology, food, busing, war, terrorism, sexism, racism, and on and on. The word is not carried on sound waves. It is by human involvement that this word spreads throughout the Garden.

Three words about us: from Eden, God's pleasure at our creation, and our wretched distortion of so good a thing; and from Bethlehem, a reconciliation that awakens the image within, freeing us from defection's control and energizing us for creative service in the Garden. Oh, that above the din of the season of much coming and going we would hear this word—about you and me.[29]

Jesus Christ, God's Son, Savior

"Be not afraid; for behold, I bring you good news of a great joy which will come to all the people; for to you is born this day in the city of David a Savior, who is Christ the Lord" (Luke 2:10-11).

The announcement of the birth of Jesus is to the shepherds. In its context, it is remarkably dramatic; but in its elaboration, it is conspicuously simple—a child is born; he is the Savior; he is Christ the Lord. Regardless of the stance we take toward this unadorned announcement as a literal account or as a statement of faith, we cannot escape its sheer surprise. After all, there is a temple at Jerusalem, and synagogues all around. There are prestigious and influential people in Bethlehem, but, wonder of wonders, it is the ears of obscure shepherds that hear the news of this great joy.

What of the city of David, far from the hub of the Roman Empire, and of only passing concern to the powers at Rome? Why Bethlehem? Luke makes little of it, but Matthew characteristically sees it as a fulfillment of ancient promise:

> "And you, O Bethlehem, in the land of Judah,
> are by no means least among the rulers of Judah;
> for from you shall come a ruler
> who will govern my people Israel."
> —Matthew 2:6

Even if connected with an old prophecy, the status of Bethlehem is unchanged. It was on the back road, obscure and insignificant; for those who sway empires have immediate and pragmatic concerns and no time for searching their destiny in the chronicles of history, especially Jewish history.

While the report is to the shepherds and is localized in Bethlehem, it is universal in scope. It is to all the people, and its appeal has no boundaries. Palestine cannot contain it. Judaism cannot define it. Eastern culture cannot imprison it.

78

The intersection of B.C. and A.D. cannot date it.

The news to shepherds for all the people, the news in Bethlehem for all the world, is that a Savior is born. He is, writes Luke, "Christ the Lord," a familiar term which New Testament scholars suggest actually represents an advanced Christology. However, later in the chapter, Luke reverts to what would have been a more acceptable formula to persons nurtured in the Hebrew faith: the Lord's Christ. That is the term used at the temple when Simeon recounts the fire in his breast that ". . . he should not see death before he had seen the Lord's Christ" (Luke 2:26). Peter's confession is, "[You are] the Christ of God" (9:20).

Luke's Christ is always the Son; God is the Father. Jesus is the beloved Son, the Chosen One, the Son of God. When Mary asks her young son why he stayed behind at the temple, the boy Jesus answers: ". . . Did you not know that I must be in my Father's house?" (2:49). At his baptism by John, Jesus hears the words of God: ". . . Thou art my beloved Son; with thee I am well pleased" (3:22). At the transfiguration Luke speaks of a cloud and a voice saying, ". . . This is my Son, my Chosen; listen to him!" (9:35).

But the humility of the shepherds, the obscurity of Bethlehem, the Christological formula are hardly the central lesson in the Lukan birth narrative. The reality that is such good news is that a Savior is born. The Christ is the Savior. That is the lesson. Matthew puts it this way: ". . . you shall call his name Jesus, for he will save his people from their sins" (Matthew 1:21).

Luke's Christ begins early to establish this sense of purpose. After the career crisis in the temptation story, Jesus goes to Galilee where his fame spreads rapidly. On Saturday, Jesus attends the synagogue as he had when growing up in Nazareth. The people, who had known him as a boy, hear him read from Isaiah:

"The Spirit of the Lord is upon me,
because he has anointed me to preach good news to the poor.
He has sent me to proclaim release to the captives

and recovering of sight to the blind,
to set at liberty those who are oppressed,
to proclaim the acceptable year of the Lord."
—Luke 4:18-19 (See also Isaiah 61:1-2.)

After the reading, he makes a bold assertion: "Today this scripture has been fulfilled in your hearing" (Luke 4:21). Later, Luke has Jesus saying, "I must preach the good news of the kingdom of God to the other cities also; for I was sent for this purpose" (4:43).

We need Luke's Savior, you and I. Here in this lovely place of worship, with the second Advent candle freshly alight, and the first still glowing, we need a Savior. The contexts from which we have come, and to which we will return today, and tomorrow, need a Savior. Persons near us who are faceless and whose names we do not know, need a Savior. The whole world needs a Savior.

The poor and the hungry in this world need Luke's Savior. In the opening line from the prophecy in Isaiah, Jesus identifies his mission as "to preach good news to the poor" (Luke 4:18). In Luke's version of the Sermon on the Plain, similar to Matthew's Sermon on the Mount, Jesus is radical in his pronouncements about the poor: "Blessed are you poor, for yours is the kingdom of God" (6:20), he says. Note that this is not the same form as in Matthew (5:3a)—"Blessed are the poor in spirit"—but "blessed are you poor." The poor belong to the kingdom of God. The story of the beggar Lazarus and the rich man (Dives) tells that upon death Lazarus goes to Abraham's bosom, but Dives goes to the abode of the dead. The rich man pleads for mercy, but the story does not yield an easy answer: ". . . Son, remember that you in your lifetime received your good things, and Lazarus in like manner evil things; but now he is comforted here, and you are in anguish" (Luke 16:25).

A ruler, asking Jesus about eternal life, was told to keep the Commandments. Smug in his reply that he had kept them from his youngest days, the man felt his confidence change to sadness when Jesus told him, "Sell all that you have and distribute to the poor . . ." (18:22). When Zacchaeus told Jesus that he had given half of his goods to the poor, Jesus said, "Today salvation has come to this house . . ." (19:9).

Similarly, Jesus was concerned with the hungry. In the Sermon on the Plain he said, "Blessed are you that hunger now, for you shall be satisfied" (6:21). Once, as he was teaching, and with suppertime approaching, Jesus felt compassion for those who had come to hear his teaching. He saw to it that they were fed.

None of us knows the solution for the shameful and complex problem of world poverty and hunger. But what we do know is that Jesus preached good news to the poor and the hungry. As followers of his, we are summoned to do something; moreover, we are accountable—under judgment. With our rationalizations and inaction, the text will not compromise.

If we are poor and hungry, do not these words of Jesus come as good news? Yes, the poor and the hungry need a Savior.

The broken and grieving of this world need Luke's Savior. *Soter*, the Greek word for savior, also means healer. Jesus healed the centurion's servant who was critically ill. He healed Simon's mother-in-law of a high fever and she got out of bed immediately and served dinner (4:38-39). He commanded unclean spirits to come out of people, comforted the grieving and raised the dead. He healed a woman with a twelve-year hemorrhage and told a man who was paralyzed to get up, take his bed in hand, and go home. He told a grieving father not to fear, as he heard of the death of the man's little girl. Going to the man's house, he took the child by the hand and told her to get up at once (8:54-55).

Would not it be wonderful if Jesus would visit our hospitals and heal the sick, or visit the homes of the confused and make them whole again, or stand beside sad persons who grieve over the death of someone close to them? That he does not do this does not mean that healing cannot take place. There are healers all around us. Daily, trained physicians diagnose and treat serious physical illnesses. Psychiatrists help persons plumb deep psychological and sometimes psycho-physiological problems to find the power to cope again with life. Certified counselors assist persons to identify and solve individual and family problems. Sensitive pastors help persons to face life's exigencies and to become whole. Even the untrained but empathetic person, through presence and words, is often able to give healing to the person who is troubled.

As for raising the dead, we run up against a solid wall. We have followed close upon too many hearses bearing someone we love, and, therefore, entertain no wishful illusions. It is painfully clear that we have not been allowed this power. As to its place in the New Testament, we will simply have to let the record stand and be astonished at its possibility.

This powerlessness notwithstanding, do we not agree that to the sick and the grieving, the words of Jesus come as hopeful news? Yes, the sick and the grieving need a Savior.

The grasping and the impatient of this world need Luke's Savior. One day the eager disciples, anticipating the reign of the Christ in his kingdom, began arguing over who would be the greatest when the kingdom came. It was a common enough concern, but Jesus gave it an uncommon resolution. Taking a child to his side, he said,

"Whoever receives this child in my name receives me, and whoever receives me receives him who sent me; for he who is least among you all is the one who is great (9:48)."

Jesus, another time, warned persons not to take the seat of honor at banquets unless they were invited to do so, for said he, "Every one who exalts himself will be humbled, and he who humbles himself will be exalted" (14:11). Luke uses this saying at the end of the account of the prayers of the ostentatious Pharisee and the humble tax collector.

Related to our penchant for grasping is our persistent impatience. The more sophisticated we become the more impatiently we behave. Luke's Jesus speaks indirectly to this problem when he teaches that the kingdom of God is like a grain of mustard seed that grows secretly and becomes a tree; and is like meal that by a maturing process becomes a loaf of bread.

We are numbered among the grasping and impatient, clambering up the ladder of success, desiring the most powerful offices, wishing for the highest degrees from the most prestigious schools, attempting to outdo our colleagues. But the greater sin is in confusing achievement with God's blessing, deluding ourselves that our grasping will earn salvation. Under such a burden, we lose perspective.

In a television drama a mother counseled her son who had given up a job in a small grocery store to go to work for a large company, where he was given a number rather than being called by a name. He was anticipating financial success and prestige. His mother warned him that he was attempting to climb an illusory mountain, which would prove to be futile, because every plateau reached would merely lure him to the next peak. "Learn to find happiness in doing what you do best," she wisely admonished the young man.

Do we not need to be reminded of the vanity of unbridled ambition? Do we not need to remember that the least will be greatest; the last, first; the humble, exalted; and that the heart should determine what is treasured; to remember that good things grow quietly and secretly, but that someday they will come to full flower? It is a difficult lesson for urbane persons, but in it is our salvation.

Do we not agree that the words of Jesus can become the hopeful news that we have listened for in our grasping and in our impatience? Yes, the grasping and the impatient need a Savior.

Luke's Jesus had a presence which drew people irresistibly to him. It was not the fabricated charisma ascribed to generals and kings or to the persuasive leader who can excite blind passion in the masses, but the attraction of wisdom and genuineness. People marvelled at his words and experienced him as real person. We cannot reenter the irreversible movement of history to meet him in the flesh, to touch and be touched, to speak to and to hear his gracious words in return. But the risen Christ is imminent, is accessible to us as he was on the Emmaus road.

To us can belong the experience of the two disciples who walked the way with him: "And their eyes were opened and they recognized him . . ." (24:31). Emmaus is a universal reality. It is here.

A resurrected Savior offers his saving presence to the poor and the hungry, to the sick and the grieving, to the grasping and the impatient. My soul, what a hopeful word; what a grand offer; my soul, what good news![30]

After Christmas

My office here at the seminary faces east and overlooks nearby shrubs and pine and oak. Farther back on the property, there is a lovely wood to stop by on a snowy day, providing a chance to resonate with the poets. Off to the left of my window is the administration building, a reminder of where I work. Covering the upper two-thirds of my window space is the all-pervasive Midwestern sky which lured our forebears from the established East to the frontier.

From this wide window, late on the Wednesday before Christmas, I watched in wonder as an easy snowfall clothed the December ground. By the time I completed the day's work and started home, there was a measurable accumulation. Trudging through the snow toward my car, I suddenly remembered a day out of the past when a storm spilled about eight inches of snow on the church parking lot and on my car. On that day in Kentucky when I left my office for home, I stepped from the back door of the church expecting some difficulty in getting to my car. But I was surprised—the church custodian had cleared a path for me and had cleaned the snow from my car. Hundreds of miles away, about eight years later, similar circumstances brought that warm memory back to me. One night at home we were viewing slides of other years. Our daughter Teresa, on seeing a picture of herself getting off the school bus on another snowy day, said, "I remember the path you cleared through the snow that day." Thus it is that the kindness we show is remembered on down through the years.

I think, however, that these vivid experiences have a broader application than just kindness, for they say to me that in spite of our despair that evil may overcome all of the good we can muster, the reality of creation is that good does and will win over evil—even though the evil looks so strong and we are so unsure about the good. How many times have we feared that the right which we have helped our children develop will be engulfed in a moment of immature passion? How many times have we shunned intellectual inquiry about the faith, for fear that the Bible or our articulation of belief will be unable to withstand? How many times have we protected the church from persons who are different from us, fearing that they can take more from us than we can allow?

Christmas means at least this: the axe has been laid to the root of evil, and though evil still pushes itself upward and outward, ensnarling a hapless humanity, it will not ultimately succeed or enjoy full influence even now. Evil will choke its victims and bruise and scratch even the innocent who wish to have no part of it. But as Martin Luther, in personalizing evil, said, "His rage we can endure, for lo, his doom is sure. . . ."[31]

In Christmas aftermath we find a hope that the constructive work we are doing is stronger than we had thought; that the might of this world which is powered by so much visible and hidden evil is after all not as strong as the quieter might which is powered by the Spirit of God; that, as one writer has said, "The good that men crave will prove stronger than evil and fear."

At least from my window here in the Midwest it looks that way.

Good Friday

One of the joys of my life is my kindergartner, Jennifer. We play games together, and we talk about everything that experience calls to mind. Being a child, she is most often on the receiving end of the teacher-learner relationship; then again, it is her "childness" that often puts her in the role of teacher.

Back before Christmas when my family and I were so sad that we could easily have foregone the usual festive aspects of the season, Jennifer brought us through. One day when I came in the front door, home for lunch, really under the load of my grief, she had the record player on, and I could hear the happy words, "'Tis the season to be jolly." She knew and felt as deeply as we the conspicuous absence in our house and the silent little secrets still in her once-shared bedroom. But she also knew how to move on with life. In the naturalness of her young years, she gave us the gift of remembering with praise and living with joy.

The other day she cut some forsythia branches to take to school. I asked her who made the beautiful yellow flowers. She said, "God." I asked her who made the nose that can smell the flowers. She said, "God." I asked her who made the blue eyes that can see the flowers. Now a little weary of my questioning, she, instead of answering, pointed upward.

Looking upward (spatially outward) for God is an indication of our incomplete understanding. However, in the ultimate sense it is a great sign of hope to a perplexed and saddened humanity. Although, when I am thinking about God as present and active in the world, I look within to the image of God that is creatively active in me. However, there are times when that will not speak to my deepest need. When I stand in lonely places in the face of irreversible realities, I find my thought, my whole being turning upward, outward toward the mystery in the spheres.

Today, in the pervasive darkness of my Good Friday, I gaze beyond the grave. Lo, there is a break, and in the break, a ray. Oh! Can it be the Easter Light?

Three Days

Black Friday—tenebrous:
    dissonance, cosmic lights hide;
    the damp, cold tomb sealed, holds
    no sign of life inside.

The Sabbath—pensive gray:
    stark silence, negative time,
    expectations darkled;
    prayers uttered without rhyme.

The Resurrection Day:
    light, life, transcendent stirring;
    death's dirge interrupted;
    joy returns, and hoping.

Easter to Eschaton:
    interim hope with reason,
    but Easter will not yield
    fruit ahead of season.

In the Breaking of Bread

Scene: The eleven and the others are in Jerusalem; Cleopas is speaking, perhaps to Mary, about what has just happened to him and an unnamed disciple, here imagined to be Samuel. (See Luke 24:13-35.)

What was Simon saying, Mary? That Jesus had appeared to him? He's right. I mean, it's true. Simon is right. Jesus is alive! That's why Samuel and I are out of breath. We were with him just this afternoon. We have practically run from Emmaus to tell you. He appeared alongside us today. We talked with him, even ate with him.

Earlier today, Samuel and I, our sadness showing in our stooped frames and measured pace, were on our way to Samuel's house at Emmaus. The awful events of the execution at Golgotha were heavy on our minds. We had passed through the Damascus Gate out of the city, making our way along the Neapolis Road as it follows the ridge northward. The anemone and other spring flowers spread their colors over the hill and roadside. Oh, we took note of their beauty, but our minds were still clouded by the ugly scenes in Jerusalem on Thursday and Friday. "Just to think, Cleopas, the soldiers ridiculed him," Samuel said, "and oh, those derisive words the rulers shouted at him."

I looked eastward, and although I could not see, I spoke of the early grain ripening in the Jordan Valley—the promise of life and eventual harvest. We took little hope in that, for death was burdensome on our hearts. I lamented to Samuel that Jesus held, in his brief days on earth, a promise like that in the fields, but to no avail. He was killed before his time, as grain cut before its blooming. How could the authorities have put to death such a wise, good man? How could they have even entertained that he was a criminal? What had he done that was so terrible? If only they could have known him in his wisdom and gentleness. If only they could have heard him penetrate to the heart of life's problems. Remember the story he used to tell about the rich man who confused his identity with the land and barns he owned? If only they could have been with him when, in the demands of the day, he stooped and held and talked to little children.

Samuel and I were actively occupied with such talk, mixed with silent moments of melancholy in the face of such absurd events. Although some pilgrims ahead of us, traveling faster than we, had already turned where the road bends, we had thought ourselves to be the only ones on the road. Then, suddenly, a stranger came alongside us. Could he have been behind us all the while, our low-hung heads not alert enough to notice? He must have been close on our heels for some time, for he perceived that we were talking about something quite important to us.

What's that, Mary? Was it Jesus? Yes, but we didn't recognize him. I mean, it was as if we were stupefied.

The stranger was forward in his manner. Without introducing himself, he asked us what we were discussing. I guess we were a little rude, for instead of introducing ourselves and greeting the stranger, we looked at him with some indignation, and I inquired, "Haven't you heard what happened in Jerusalem this week? Man, where have you been?" Although he did not answer yes or no, he did ask me what I meant.

Well, although I was not as curt as before, I replied, "No doubt you have heard of Jesus, a teacher from Nazareth who became a prophet among us, performing miracles and teaching wisely. To put it mildly, his teachings and activities were so threatening to the religious authorities that they conspired to have him brought to trial before Pilate. Last Friday, the Roman soldiers executed him. We were among his disciples, and, as you can imagine, we had high hopes that he would be Israel's Savior. But, look, it has been three days. We are confused and disconsolate. But, then, why am I confessing our feelings to you? You only asked a simple question of fact."

That's right, Mary, I stood there telling Jesus all about himself, not knowing, not seeing who he was. Looking back now, it's unbelievable.

At this point, Samuel and I were utterly astonished. Scanning the valley below the ridge, the stranger changed his gait and spoke to us. Although he had overtaken us along the road, we found ourselves falling in step with his pace and listening.

What's that, Mary, did he tell us who he was? No! And we still had no idea, I mean, how could we? Well, looking back now, he looked like Jesus, but, as I said before, we— Samuel and I, Cleopas, who had sat at his feet so many times and heard his words—didn't know who he was. I can't understand it. He was right there next to me; I heard his voice. But I didn't know that it was Jesus.

Not only did the stranger change our pace, he also took charge of the conversation. He turned out to be a religious man. In fact, he gave Samuel and me a mild scolding. At least, I felt rebuked when he asked a cutting question, "Brothers, why are you so slow to believe what the prophets proclaimed? Didn't you know that the Christ had to suffer to enter into glory?"

With his question, both Samuel and I raised our bodies to full stature. Our blood boiled. Besides being forward, he was also presumptuous. I retorted, "Friend, who do you think you are? We were followers of Jesus, but we've never seen you before. Have you eaten with him as we have? What gives you the right to talk to us this way? Further, how came you to know about the hopes and prophets of Israel?"

Again the stranger scanned the countryside, as if to ignore my challenge. He didn't answer my question, at least not directly. Rather, he went on instructing us. Only this time, he didn't merely sound like a religious person, he spoke as a wise teacher. My defenses were coming down. He talked of Jesus and of God's plan from the time of Moses to now. He put it all into perspective.

This stranger seemed to understand the very heart of God as he told of God's pity for the Hebrews in Egypt's grip. I wish you could have seen the resolution in his face when he recounted how God had called Moses to tell the elders of Israel, "I have observed you and what has been done to you in Israel." I wish you could have seen how animated he became when he spoke of God's expectation that people "do justice, love kindness, and walk humbly." For some unexplainable reason, upon hearing these words, I remembered Jesus' sensitivities to the captive, the hungry, the oppressed.

Suddenly, the man's countenance took a special hue, his voice a more intimate timbre, as he spoke of the Suffering Servant in Isaiah. I wondered why he stared at his own open hands as he began reciting the poem, his eyes at times glancing, his head almost turning back toward Jerusalem. In a moment of deep inwardness, he started quoting a psalm, "My God, my God, why hast thou forsaken me." But, he quickly came back to himself and continued with his insights.

Yes, Mary, I know. We should have known by then who he was. But, I tell you, we just could not break through that mysterious barrier between us. The experience was like being in a place you feel you have been before but somehow cannot identify.

His teaching was so arresting that it seemed to me we had walked only a short distance from the city; but in fact, we were at Emmaus, with Samuel's house in sight. The stranger stopped talking; he didn't press us to see if we understood. Without a word, he looked straight into our eyes, paused for a moment as if he knew us, then stepped out ahead of us, as though some purpose were leading him past Emmaus. I should have known by his eyes; eyes are always betrayers of identity.

Samuel put his hand on my shoulder and whispered to me, "I've never heard such wisdom. Even our Lord didn't tell us these things when he taught us. I'm going to invite him to supper; we are almost home. Besides, it's toward evening, and he'll need a place to sleep."

After settling in at Samuel's house, we sat down for supper, and the stranger did it again. He took the initiative. Remember, on the road, he came up from behind us, but we soon found ourselves following him. We told him about the events of the week in Jerusalem, but he told us what it all meant. We were two of Jesus' disciples attempting to tell him about Jesus, but he dominated the conversation, giving us perspectives we had never known before. And then, at supper at Samuel's table, he took over again. He lifted the bread, blessed it, and passed it to us.

It was then, Mary, it was then. It was a most intriguing and puzzling experience. It was when he served the bread. He pulled the bread apart; looked directly into our eyes, as he had on the road, only this time he called us by name—"Samuel, Cleopas," he said—as he passed the bread. Then it happened. We recognized him. The stranger was Jesus. It was in the breaking of bread, Mary, the breaking of bread. As we held the bread in our hands, our eyes were opened; in the breaking of bread, we saw the risen Christ.[32]

Hoping, in the
Creative Interim

Hoping, in the Creative Interim

On the afterside of Easter we know that our desperation cannot be assumed with airtight logic or given over to irreversibility. On this side, we have learned that what seems to be is not always what is. The darkest night has a morning; the most imprisoning experience, an escape; the most desperate of problems, a solution; the most violent of storms, a passing. Easter has taught us the arrogance of our presumption that all is lost.

Yet, our after-Easter experience is still subject to a cataract of black Fridays. The Christ has been raised, but still sealed are the graves that you and I watch over. Still heavy are the chains of injustice that fetter much of the world day after weary day. Still long are the moments of suffering borne by persons caught in the throes of tragedy. Easter will not bear its fruit ahead of time!

Easter introduces into the arena of existence the renewed possibility of transcendence. Though the grave be covered over with grass, there is now in the psyche the freshly disclosed word that at work is a reality higher than that which the eyes behold or the memory educes. Though the bounds of our lives are narrowly defined by harsh and fickle realities, we begin to see that the boundaries are temporal and weaker than the creative energy of God.

Thus are the Fridays of after-Easter both "black" and "good." The paradox of our finitude and transcendence is our companion for life. We are persistently caught in the tension which these polarities produce. Until the last fruits of the resurrection are yielded, you and I live in the interim. It is the strength of the promise that makes it endurable.

To endure in the interim does not mean that we must stand passively before reality. To do so would be to have a woefully stagnant existence. What follows is a vision of creative hoping—in the interim between the promise and the fulfillment.

Keeping Joy Alive

There are three joys and three conditions under which joy lives. There is a waking joy, a walking joy, and an evening joy. There is a joy because of, a joy in spite of, and a joy in promise of.

Waking joy is a joy that anticipates. It comes as a burst of energy or a sudden alertness to what is around us. It breaks in on our perceptions and shapes our perspectives. It is that presence that we feel when, on a spring morning, the birdsong and the dawning awaken us. It is then that we realize that we have been given another day, a gift which comes entirely without our effort. We accept it and anticipate how we might live in it. This waking joy might even be visceral, as in the excitement of the athlete on the day of an important contest. It brings out the child in us, an intriguing behavior which I saw in some colleagues on the day of a faculty retreat. On the way to the campus to load the vans, a colleague passed me in his car. Instead of the usual routine wave of his hand, he lifted his fishing rod, shaking it with a message. Another associate, once we arrived on the retreat grounds, became almost ecstatic when he saw the putting greens.

There is a walking joy, a joy in participation. This is a total experience and more lasting than the anticipatory joy. It comes in an intimate moment with one's lover, an enthralling moment in a forest giving way to autumn, in the reading of favorite Scriptures and books. A friend of mine found this joy in his daughter's diverse activities in school. As she played in sports, he was her foremost cheerleader; in stage productions, he was the first to shout, "Bravo!" Watching our children mature and achieve is, indeed, an unequaled walking joy.

There is an evening joy, a joy in remembering. This joy may not be as visceral or as total as walking joy. It is not a stirring joy that calls us to action, nor is it a joy that accompanies participation. It is a quiet joy, and its effect is a healthy acceptance and sense of peace. It must be the joy that accompanies old age when a person, beyond the passions of youth and the strivings of middle age, takes in life fully. But, being retrospective, it need not be reserved for the end of life. I have come to the end of a day of productive writing, sat down on the back porch, and remembered in joy the experience of the day.

Joy is experienced under three conditions—joy because of, joy in spite of, and joy in promise of. While waiting for my car to be repaired at a local shop, I noted the unusual liveliness of the junior mechanic. His behavior was so conspicuous— he whistled, he skipped from one place to the next, and his eyes had a special gleam—that it required a query, "Why are you so happy today?" I learned that he had just found a valued car part for only fifty dollars. His eyes danced as he answered, showing the prize to me. His joy in the car part made no sense and had no value to me, but I experienced joy because of his delight. The mechanic's joy and mine, after his, were joys because of.

There is a joy in spite of. Personal circumstances regarding family, health, work, and economics are thieves of joy. How stealthily they enter our lives and empty us of all pleasure unless we find joy in spite of pain. My friends told me about a local couple who lost two children in death, then, after running their grief process to its full cycle, adopted a child. Theirs is a model for an active pursuit of joy in spite of circumstances. Surely they knew the line given by George Matheson, "O Joy that seekest me through pain, I cannot close my heart to thee."[33]

There is a joy in promise of. Few people are strangers to the pain of separation which puts an edge on joy. Most of us have lonely places where we stand between the shadow of death and the Easter Light. We know the agony of unresolved ultimate questions. Thus we take inward journeys until we stand between the vision and the reality, and we wonder. And there we find joy, because there we touch an everlasting promise, a pledge that what has been begun will be completed. God said, "Tell my people Israel that I hear their groanings and that I will deliver them" (see Exodus 3:7-8). Jesus said, "I will be with you" (see Matthew 28:20). Matheson's verse continues: "I trace the rainbow thro' the rain, And feel the promise is not vain That morn shall tearless be."[34]

These joys of which I speak are kept alive through experience, but running throughout this process of "joying" is a perspective, a guiding vision which overtook me in my mid-thirties. In an undated moment, I came to see that a creating God was still at work in the world and was calling me to be a creative trustee in the world. I suddenly understood at the depth of intellect and heart that it was now my time in the life cycle and in the history of the race to join the generational stream as a primary giver. I became, in Erikson's terms, a generative adult; in my own terms, a creative trustee.[35]

This creating God, who calls us, came before all that is, came before us, and will always be. The God we worship and who calls us has never not been and will never not be. There has never been a time when we could talk of the God who someday would be, and there will never be a time when we will talk of the God who was. The God who eternally is, has been clearly shown in Jesus Christ, a man in time who puts us in touch with time-transcendence, a man in humanity who leads us in creation's fulfillment in resurrection.

This perspective extends to my ministry, to my social relations, to my family life, to my diversions. It permeates my being and my relationships. It keeps joy alive in me—the waking joy, the walking joy, the evening joy—the joy because of, the joy in spite of, the joy in promise of.

Celebrating the Moment

A winter day spent by the fire, with a view through windowpanes to the falling snow offers an illusion of eternity. Thus is it a stay against impermanence. However, the snowflake in the palm will not grant our wish for it to stay. Though downy flake piles upon downy flake to make a wonderland of our otherwise barren yards and woods, the snow cannot stay. As it is with the snow that will not forever linger, so it is with life. We have sought permanence and instead have learned the folly of the search.

The little girl creating images in the snow will, with her creations, also go away, for childhood turns into adolescence, and youth yields to adulthood. The birds visiting at the feeder outside the kitchen window will not stay. The warm fire on the hearth will burn itself away. The long respite of the winter day, however savored by solitude, good company, and steaming brew, will end. Thus, does it fall to us to embrace our transient nature, to celebrate fully the moment that is before us, knowing that in the authentic moment we are experiencing the dynamics of the ultimately eternal.

It is no easy matter, for we appear most often to be holding on to some experience gone or reaching for some reality out ahead of us. Remembering and anticipating, except as they are connected in integrity with the present moment, are dangling realities. In our company are pitiable persons whose life stories are but yesterdays and others whose myths are but idle wishes for tomorrow.

A middle-aged man once was very successful with a carmaker in Detroit, but he had fallen from executive grace. He talked of his former exploits as if the intervening decade had not passed. He seemed most alive in those moments, but when present experience was the agenda, he was cynical, bitter, hostile, and divisive. A younger friend talked often of the book he was going to write, tomorrow; but the pages of that dream remain blank and crumpled beside a dusty typewriter. The twin plights are interwoven in the person of Delta Dawn, a person in a popular song. She wears an old rose from the fantasized past and waits for an illusory lover who will deliver her from melancholy and restore her happiness. There are in these persons no throbbing, hands-on reality, no presence to the good moment in which they dwell.

Involved in this grasping of the moment is a perspective that might be termed "life calls to life." I came across it in the mid-1970s after two sad visits to Tennessee to bury my brothers, who had died within a few months of each other. They were the last of my four brothers, and at their burials I visited again the graves of my parents, grandparents, aunts and uncles, and other persons who framed my growing up in our little community in the hills. Death was all around, but I was struck by the notion that despite death, life calls to life. Although there are times when it seems that the whole world is dying, life calls us to live.

As we, our relatives, and our friends grow older, we will see and feel the pain of death all around us. Enacted before our very eyes will be the truth that life moves toward death. If we allow that perspective to shape the central theme of our existence, we will wither away in despair, and every day will be a dying. It is true that life moves toward death, but the greater reality is that life calls to life. And here is the secret which Jesus lived and which we can so easily miss. The present moment is pregnant with the eternal if we will but be midwife to its birth.

You and I have this moment together. Its measure is in its quality, not its length or even its ultimate destiny. Here is where the dimensions of the eternal are first experienced. It is this truth that came to me as I mused upon a sad visit to my native Tennessee.

Celebrating the present moment also involves recognizing the particularity of experience, understanding that our experiences, like photographs, are but imprints of reality. Such an awareness was mine on a plane trip from Kansas City to Atlanta. Traveling by air is not my highest joy, but when distance and allotted time require it, I can enjoy the flight. At heights too great to contemplate, one views earth's plane and sees, as miniatures, the cars, homes, and trees below. The observation of how small we creatures and our comforts appear from a higher vantage is an often told lesson, but I have a different lesson to tell.

Recently in flying over the lakes and ponds in the outstate, I experienced a theophany of sorts. When the angle of incidence of the sun's reflection met my eyes, the waters below suddenly burst with light and then as suddenly lost their radiance. I've lost myself on such fare for as long as there was water and sun, anticipating the momentary glow of each little bowl of water, then savoring it until it recedes from my consciousness.

The last time this pleasure was mine it came to me that we are like these waters. Most of our days are spent serving our purpose, fulfilling our essence without dramatic evidence of the eternal which energizes and illumines us. Then suddenly the angle of reflection is just right and we see—however momentarily—the light of God in each other, and we call each other "Thou."

Such authentic experiences are gifts. They come as surprises from the most mundane of circumstances. They are hedges against transience and irrationality. They shed fresh perspectives on our conflicts and disappointments. They bring us a feeling of being at one with the wider flow of reality. Like a deep breath, they put us at ease. For the hoping interim, these brief particularizations of transcendence are something to hold to and to be held by.

Worshiping in Community

Again and again, it is my experience that worship in community is the central event of the church. Worship is the discerning and energizing center for my existence in the creative interim between the promise and the fulfillment of resurrection. In the Advent candles, the Easter alleluias, and the Supper, within a community of believers, there is strength and meaning. There is hoping.

Once, during a critical point in my career, I learned again the lesson of Advent. Some readers of my books had found ideas in my writings that they considered dangerous for the good of the gospel. As will happen, they were joined by others who, perhaps without becoming readers, took up the concern. Swiftly, then, concern moved to cause, and cause to battle, and I found myself in the uneasy circle of controversy. As colleagues, students, graduates, and other friends heard of the matter, they wrote and called, expressing a wide range of emotions. One caller in particular inquired of me whether I would be staying or going, for he wanted to offer his support and considerable influence should I feel it was time for me to go. My reply came without forethought, and I look back on it as an experience of hope: "I don't know just now; I'm waiting for the lighting of the first Advent candle."

It was Holy Week 1970. The Crescent Hill Baptist Church had endured a long winter of suffering and tragedy; had prayed only to find its prayers not answered; had hoped, only to find its spirit disappointed; had held to the life of a little girl, only finally having to give in to the course of events beyond its control. As the week moved toward its end, there was a pervasive sense of anticipation of Easter Sunday. It was not the anticipation of hilarity, with ostentatious displays of emotion, but an expectation expressed in quiet terms of hope as we whispered to each other, "We are waiting for Easter." Then came the day, and the congregation stood for the hymn of praise to sing an Easter alleluia. These sounds reverberate yet, for they are ultimate and real, and they keep hope alive in the interim.

My pastor, Lee Stephens, values the place of the Lord's Supper in the church's worship. Thus does the congregation participate in it as a pivotal experience of worship. Whenever upon entering the sanctuary I see the bread and trays, my adrenalin flows, because for me the Supper has come to be a tangible experience in which my humanity and transcendence join. As our congregation partakes of the material elements, we actualize the communion which we have with each other and we symbolize the great hope-fulfilled community in which the risen Christ will pass the cup of blessing.

On countless Sundays and Holy Thursdays, the Supper has imparted sustenance and renewal and kept hope alive.

Listening to the Silence

The reader who has stayed with me through the sermons, the prose, and the poems has taken note of my allusions and references to the deaths of Laura Lue Claypool and our daughter Laura Suzanna. If such has been to excess, ascribe it to the pervasive effect these absurdities have had on my mind and heart. The plain truth is that no year has shaped my hoping as fully as the one in which these two beautiful and innocent children were buried. Please indulge me two more moments.

William E. Hull preached, in his usual eloquent way, the sermon for Laura Lue. He spoke of how God embraces us in our silence in the face of death, and he made reference to the half hour of silence in heaven when the seventh seal was opened. A close friend of the family, he was at the Claypool's home when the end came. He closed the sermon with these hopeful words:

> The silence lasted "for about half an hour" as the family said goodbye. When they came down, there was really nothing to say, nor is there now. Except that the seemingly endless half hour of silence is in heaven, too. And I knew that afternoon that the silence could be endured. For the silence belongs to God.[36]

Faye, Teresa, Jennifer, and I moved from Louisville to Kansas City in the summer of 1972. My first visit back to Louisville was in late October, when the area was graced with autumn's artistry and ambience. Autumn's painting, inspiring in its beauty, could not hold back melancholy. I celebrated the beauty, as in years past, but needed no encouragement to be pensive, for Laura Suzanna's grave lay before me. Kneeling, I rubbed my fingers across the etchings on the gravestone, perhaps unconsciously searching for some brailled cosmic words to heal the pain. I cried and waited in the silence. At first, hearing only memories, my ears were suddenly tuned to the October breeze, which hitherto had not been apparent.

It filtered gently through the trees, carrying and rustling the falling and fallen leaves. Against an unaccountable chill over me, I pulled my sweater tighter about, for in the hush the wind carried Easter stirrings.

G. Jermyn Sparkman

Notes

1. Walter Chalmers Smith, from the hymn "Immortal, Invisible, God Only Wise."
2. Isaac Watts, from the hymn "O God, Our Help in Ages Past."
3. William E. Henley, "Invictus," in John Connell, *W. E. Henley* (Port Washington, N.Y.: Kennikat Press, 1972), p. 4.
4. Sermon preached in July 1971 at Crescent Hill Baptist Church, Louisville, Kentucky, a year after Laura Suzanna's death.
5. Except where noted, the poems in this sermon are the author's.
6. This legend is a creation of the author.
7. Robert Frost, "A Question," *Complete Poems of Robert Frost* (New York: Holt, Rinehart and Winston, 1967), p. 493. Quoted from *The Poetry of Robert Frost* edited by Edward Connery Latham. Copyright © 1942 by Robert Frost. Copyright © 1969 by Holt, Rinehart and Winston. Copyright © 1970 by Lesley Frost Ballantine. Reprinted by permission of Holt, Rinehart and Winston, Publishers.
8. Archibald MacLeish, *J.B.: A Play in Verse* (Boston: Houghton Mifflin Company, 1958), p. 152. Copyright © 1956, 1957, 1958 by Archibald MacLeish. Reprinted by permission of Houghton Mifflin Company.
9. Plato, *Phaedo*, in *Great Books of the Western World*, ed. Robert Maynard Hutchins, trans. Benjamin Jowett (Chicago: Encyclopaedia Brittanica, Inc., 1952), pp. 250 and 251.
10. Sermon allegory preached at Midwestern Seminary Chapel, Kansas City, Missouri, 1981.
11. Rupert Brooke, "The Dead," *The Collected Poems of Rupert Brooke* (New York: Dodd, Mead and Company, 1915), p. 110.
12. Gordon Lightfoot, "The Wreck of the Edmund Fitzgerald." Copyrighted by Morse Music, a Division of EMP Ltd. 1976.
13. William Cullen Bryant, "Thanatopsis," *Poems of William Cullen Bryant* (London: Oxford University Press, 1914), p. 13.
14. John R. Claypool, *Tracks of a Fellow Struggler* (Waco, Tex.: Word Books, 1974), p. 39.
15. Richard Bach, *Jonathan Livingston Seagull* (New York: Macmillan, Inc., 1970), p. 27.
16. Homer, *The Iliad*, in *Great Books of the Western World*, ed. Robert Maynard Hutchins, trans. Samuel Butler (Chicago: Encyclopaedia Brittanica, Inc., 1952), p. 8.
17. John H. Newman, from the hymn "Lead, Kindly Light."
18. Sermon preached at Midwestern Seminary Chapel, Kansas City, Missouri, 1974.
19. William Shakespeare, *Hamlet*, in *The Complete Works of William Shakespeare* (New York: Anvel Books, 1975), p. 1088.
20. William Shakespeare, *Macbeth*, in *The Complete Works of William Shakespeare* (New York: Anvel Books, 1975), p. 1068.
21. *The Epic of Gilgamesh*, ed. Betty Radice and Robert Baldick (Baltimore: Penguin Books Inc., 1971), p. 92.

22. *Ibid.*, p. 104.
23. Archibald MacLeish, *J.B.: A Play in Verse* (Boston: Houghton Mifflin Company, 1958), p. 123. Copyright © 1956, 1957, 1958 by Archibald MacLeish. Reprinted by permission of Houghton Mifflin Company.
24. *Ibid.*
25. Martin Luther King, Jr., "I Have a Dream," *Negro Protest Thought in the Twentieth Century*, ed. Francis L. Broderick and August Meier (New York: The Bobbs-Merrill Company, Inc., 1965), p. 403.
26. Carlyle Marney, *Priests to Each Other* (Valley Forge: Judson Press, 1974), p. 89.
27. *The Epic of Gilgamesh*, pp. 96, 97.
28. Sermon preached at Midwestern Seminary Chapel, Kansas City, Missouri, 1978.
29. Midwestern Seminary *Spire*, Kansas City, Missouri, 1975.
30. Sermon preached at Wornall Road Baptist Church, Kansas City, Missouri, Advent 1982.
31. Martin Luther, from the hymn "A Mighty Fortress Is Our God."
32. The author gratefully acknowledges the assistance of reference librarian Larry McKinney and archeologist-professor William Morton, both of the Midwestern Baptist Seminary staff, for critical and contextual assistance with this sermon.
33. George Matheson, from the hymn "O Love That Wilt Not Let Me Go."
34. *Ibid.*
35. This idea is developed in my book *The Salvation and Nurture of the Child of God* (Valley Forge: Judson Press, 1983).
36. William E. Hull, "The Sound of Silence," from a sermon preached at Crescent Hill Baptist Church, Louisville, Kentucky, January 1970.